Look Smarter Than You Are with Essbase Studio 11

Updated for 11.1.2.2

Glenn Schwartzberg

2nd Edition

interRel Press, Arlington, Texas

Look Smarter Than You Are with Essbase Studio 11

Glenn Schwartzberg

Published by:
> interRel Press
> A Division of interRel Consulting Partners
> Suite 304
> 1000 Ballpark Way
> Arlington, TX 76011

All rights reserved. No portion of this book may be reproduced or transmitted in any form or by any means, electronic or mechanical, including photocopying, recording or duplication by any information storage retrieval system without the express written consent of the author or interRel Press except for the inclusion of brief quotations in a review.

Copyright © 2012-Present By Glenn Schwartzberg
2st edition
Printed in the United States of America

Library of Congress Cataloging-in-Publication Data
Schwartzberg, Glenn
> Look Smarter Than You are with Essbase Studio 11

Glenn Schwartzberg 2nd ed.
> p. 251 cm.
> Includes index.
> ISBN 978-1-105-66215-7

Trademarks
Various trademarked names appear throughout this book. Rather than list all the names and the companies/individuals that own those trademarks or try to insert a trademark symbol every time a trademarked name is mentioned, the author and publisher state that they are using the names only for editorial purposes and to the benefit of the trademark owner with no intention of trademark infringement.

This book is dedicated to all of the people who have given me help through my career. This is one way I can play that help forward and assist others. I would especially like to thank my wife and children who put up with my odd sense of humor.

As William Shakespeare said
"All the world's a stage,
And all the men and women merely players:
They have their exits and their entrances;"

We all play our parts and I hope mine is helpful to others.

Glenn Schwartzberg

ABOUT THE AUTHOR

Glenn Schwartzberg has been an IT professional for over 30 years, yet he still knows very little. He really does not exist but is a pseudonym for Johnny Depp, who does not want anyone to know he has a technical background. (Anyone believe this?)

Glenn started his career in IT (then MIS) working on IBM mainframes writing COBOL and CICS programs. He quickly worked his way up the food chain and as a manager had 15 people working for him. At this pivotal juncture, he decided he would rather be a technical resource vs. spending his time telling other people what to do and justify his life through paperwork (Editor's Note by T. McMullen: As Director of Consulting Services for interRel, are you saying I justify my life through paperwork?).

Because of this ideal, he entered the world of consulting where he became a DBA on Teradata DBC1012 computers, programming and maintaining databases. This was his introduction to SQL. During his stint working on data warehouses, he ran into a little program from Arbor software called Essbase. It was a cool application and Glenn immediately saw the value in allowing users to get their own data, so he started learning all he could about it. This was on version 3.11. As time and versions progressed, he learned more and more and the versions got more feature rich and complicated.

Glenn did feel it important to assist others as they tried to figure out the issues they were having with the application. He joined bulletin boards and forums and was an ardent contributor, answering others' questions and gaining more knowledge.

In 2008, due to his continued efforts to assist others and to evangelize Essbase, he was honored with the title of Oracle Ace in BI. In 2010, he was privileged to be named an Oracle Ace Director. He continues to share his knowledge of Essbase and its associated products though the Oracle EPM Discussion Forums, presentations at conferences, user group meetings, webcasts, and the blog he writes (it has the longest name in history): http://glennschwartzbergs-essbase-blog.blogspot.com/.

He was one of its founding members and currently sits on the Oracle Database Tools User Group (ODTUG) Hyperion Sig board.

When he is not busy serving as a Sr. Architect for interRel Consulting, he spends his free time with his lovely wife Delona, his favorite (only) daughter Tammy and volunteering with the American Youth Soccer Organization (AYSO) refereeing youth soccer matches.

ABOUT THE SENIOR EDITOR

Tracy McMullen, Oracle ACE Director, has been leading the development of Enterprise Performance Management and Data Warehousing applications for over 10 years. Roles on projects have ranged from developer to architect and project manager on technologies from Hyperion and Business Objects to Cognos and Oracle. She's seen all of the business intelligence tools and Hyperion is her favorite.

Tracy started her career at Arthur Andersen Business Consulting on a project programming in RPG (fun stuff!). Thankfully, her next project introduced her to the world of multi-dimensional databases with a Cognos PowerPlay implementation for an oil and gas client. (Many years ago Tracy was certified in Cognos PowerPlay and Impromptu). Next, she helped clients from various industries revolutionize their information delivery with Hyperion and other technologies. After years of successful business intelligence implementations, a few shredded documents changed her career path from future Partner to eliminating cancer.

Tracy joined The University of Texas M.D. Anderson Cancer Center, where she led the charge in implementing budget and planning solutions utilizing Hyperion Planning. Fate stepped in once again with relocation to the South Texas Coast and Tracy found her new home with interRel Consulting as Director of Consulting Services.

Tracy is a Hyperion Certified Consultant for Hyperion Essbase, Hyperion Certified Solutions Architect for Hyperion Planning and a Certified Project Management Professional (PMP). She assisted Oracle in the development of the new Oracle 11 Essentials exams for implementation specialists in Hyperion Planning, Essbase and Financial Management. Tracy has been a regular instructor at interRel, user conferences and other professional seminars since 2000 on topics including information delivery, business intelligence, data warehousing, and Hyperion implementations. Her strong technical background is complemented by comprehensive practical experience in project management, a skill important not only on the job but at home as well where she manages her kids on a daily basis (okay, she attempts to manage with moderate success).

ABOUT INTERREL CONSULTING

Integrated solutions are key to providing our clients the timely information they need to make critical business decisions. Our philosophy, experience, and methodologies are integral components of our application development, project management, optimization and training. As a result of our experience and commitment to excellence, interRel has become one of the premier providers of analytical solutions using Oracle BI and Hyperion solutions.

interRel solves business problems through utilizing Business Intelligence (BI) and Enterprise Performance Management (EPM) technologies. Our EPM Assessment is designed to identify an organization's current EPM current state relative to the corporate strategy.

interRel has been in business since 1997, and we take pride in delivering our solutions with small teams composed of members with an average of over eight years of Oracle Hyperion and BI related tools, application and consulting experience.

Exclusive EPM/BI consultancy

- 100% of revenue is Oracle EPM / BI-Derived
- 100% of Consultants specialize in Oracle EPM System/Hyperion
- 100% of Senior Consultants are Hyperion Certified
- Senior Consultants have 8+ years of experience
- Junior Consultants have 5+ years of experience

Oracle Hyperion Community - Training, Free Webcasts, and More

Through our various outlets, our focus is always to interact and help others in the Oracle Hyperion community.

If you like this book, join us in person for a hands-on training class. interRel Consulting offers classroom education on a full spectrum of EPM/BI solutions, including standard course offerings such as *Essbase and Planning Accelerated Fundamentals*, tailored for new Administrators as well as unique advanced courses like *Essbase Calc Scripts for Mere Mortals*. All classes are taught by knowledgeable, certified trainers whose experience combines to an average of 8+ years. This interactive environment allows attendees the opportunity to master the skill sets needed to implement, develop and manage EPM/BI solutions successfully. All classes are held at headquarters in Dallas and offer CPE accreditation. interRel Consulting also provides custom training to clients.

interRel Consulting proudly offers free weekly webcasts. These webcasts include the full scope of Oracle BI and EPM System (Hyperion) products, including Essbase, Planning & HFM. Webcasts are primarily held every non-holiday week and twice in most weeks. Topics include 'Tips, Tricks & Best Practices,' which gives you an insider's guide to optimize the usage of your solution. The 'Administration' series focuses on making your job easier and giving a snapshot of the Accelerated Fundamentals course outline while the 'Overview' webcasts discuss the highlights of a solution and how it can be used effectively. All webcasts include interactive examples and demonstrations to see how the products really work.

Awards & Recognitions

- 2008 and 2009 Oracle Titan Award winner for "EPM and BI Solution" of the year
- 2008 Oracle Excellence Award winner with Pearson Education
- 2009 Oracle Innovation Award in BI & EPM winner
- 2011 - interRel received honorable mentions in both the "Financial Management & EPM" and "Energy & Utilities Industry" categories
- Inc. magazine's 5000 fastest-growing private companies in the country (AKA: "Inc. 5000.") – 2008, 2009, 2010 and 2011
- The only Hyperion consulting partner with three Oracle ACE Directors

interRel's commitment to providing our customers with unsurpassed customer service and unmatched expertise make interRel the partner of choice for a large number of companies across the world. To learn more, visit **www.interrel.com**.

ACKNOWLEDGEMENTS

I would like to thank the academy for this award. It means you like me, you really like me. Oh wait, wrong person, wrong speech. In reality, I would like to thank Edward and Tracy for putting up with my bizarre sense of humor (lack of humor) and ramblings and their faith in me to produce a book of the same caliber as they would have written themselves. They did have to edit almost every paragraph I wrote in order to make it comprehensible.

I want to thank one of the hardest nose editors I've ever encountered (even though this is my first book). Vanessa Roske was tireless and caught countless grammar and punctuation errors in the first two drafts of the book. If you ever need an editor who can be mercilessly straightforward/cruel in her commentary, e-mail her at mycroftrholmes@gmail.com. She should charge far more than she does for her amazing editing skills.

I also would like to thank my close friend Cameron Lackpour who spent countless personal hours going through the text and going step-by-step through all the exercises. Without his expert help, you would be very confused when going through the book. While I'm not going to pay him for this, I will give him a 20% discount on the final version of the book and I won't charge him for signing his copy!

If I were to thank all of those who assisted us in the creation of this book, I would have to not only personally mention hundreds of people but they would want me to pay them for their assistance and that is NOT going to happen.

DISCLAIMER

This book is designed to provide supporting information about the related subject matter. It is being sold to you and/or your company with the understanding that the author and the publisher are not engaged by you to provide legal, accounting, or any other professional services of any kind. If assistance is required (legal, expert, or otherwise), seek out the services of a competent professional such as a consultant.

It is not the purpose of this book to reprint all of the information that is already available on the subject at hand. The purpose of this book is to complement and supplement other texts already available to you. For more information (especially including technical reference information), please contact the software vendor directly or use your on-line help.

Great effort has been made to make this book as complete and accurate as possible. That said, there may be errors both typographic and in content. As such, use this book only as a general guide and not as the ultimate source for specific information on the software product. Further, this book contains information on the software that was generally available as of the publishing date.

The purpose of this book is to entertain while educating. The author and interRel Press shall have neither liability nor responsibility to any person living or dead or entity currently or previously in existence with respect to any loss or damage caused or alleged to be caused directly, indirectly, or otherwise by the information contained in this book.

If you do not wish to abide by all parts of the above disclaimer, please stop reading now and return this book to the publisher for a full refund.

FORWARD AND FOREWARNED

This book is intended to be a companion to the highly successful *Look Smarter than You Are with Essbase 11: An Administrator's Guide*. Knowledge and concepts presented in that book are critical to understanding the content of this book. Of course, this knowledge can be substituted with a prerequisite knowledge of Essbase in general. Though as a warning, some of the jokes in this book relate to the original book series and the authors (juggling wolverines, Fight Club references). It is not important to get or understand the humor from that book nor is it important to understand why this book is humorless! What is important is to understand the concepts and process this book attempts to impart upon you the reader. Well, not really. What is important is for me to actually get published so I can have my 15 minutes of fame.

In order to effectively use this book and replicate the examples, you must have the following steps in place:
1. Working Essbase instance
2. Installed Essbase Studio
3. Have a relational source with the sample tables created and populated. Use the SQL code found in the <path>D:\Oracle\Middleware\EPMSystem11R1\products \Essbase\EssbaseStudio\Server\sqlscripts directory for the relational database of your choice.

You also, of course, have to have provisioned yourself with enough access in Shared Services to actually create Essbase databases and to create models in Essbase Studio. This book will not go over the install of any products but will concentrate on the real creation of models. Don't you feel god-like just hearing that you are the creator?

The pictures and descriptions are based on Studio 11.1.2 and in some cases 11.1.2.2 because features and functionality were greatly enhanced from the 11.1.1.X releases; if you are using an earlier version (or later) you may not have the same functionality as what you see in the book.

Any likeness to a person real or imagined is a coincidence. I have to say that so I can't get sued, you might find similarities to some real characters I know.

Table of Contents

Chapter 1:
The Plot Sickens

It was a typical day here at Essbase Studio; we had been editing dailies and drinking our lunches out of paper bags when in walked this cocky Hollywood type. You know - scruffy beard, self-indulged, smelling of cheese, curds and tofu. Must be a vegan, I thought. Of course I was wrong, not about him being a vegan, but about the smell of cheese as I was later reminded vegans don't eat cheese. He introduced himself as ER. These egocentric stars always think initials or one name is good enough.

At first I blew him off, but then he started talking about a project that caught my imagination. The premise was something about juggling wolverines. I didn't know if he was talking about football players, X-Men or wild animals, but it sounded interesting. He'd been doing it for a while and wanted to chronicle and analyze the profitability of the endeavor. (Seems his biggest expense was medical; who would have thought?) He had been loading his data from customers and suppliers into Essbase manually from flat files and wanted to make the process more robust, as this had grown into a multi-million dollar enterprise. That is, he wanted to make the process more automated, add the ability to load from his relational wolverine database and get back to the detailed information in his database. That got my attention - both the money and the need. This was right up our alley; Essbase Studio was designed to do all he wanted and more.

I decided that while he might be a snot nosed punk, this project had potential. More importantly, he had money. About this time, in walked a toothpick of a girl. He introduced her as "Tracy – best co-author ever". I quickly figured out that she was the brains behind the project, so I showed ER where to find the nuts and grains on the Kraft food table and left him to graze while Tracy and I went off to discuss the details of the project. Tracy was the full package, an intelligent pretty lady. Problem was, she was all business. She wanted to know all about Essbase Studio before she would buy in. I mean I couldn't just give her a little song and dance; I had to do the whole tour. It was time to call the "special" tram for a behind the scenes tour of the studio. This was going to be a tour like no one had seen before, visiting every department from the archives, to see the studio history, all the way to animation at the end. This was going to be one tough assignment, but if we could pull it off (and I knew we could) there would be wolverines juggled all over the big screen. I went over the tour with ER and Tracy. (I found out his real name was pretty boring - Edward Roske. "Okay," I thought, "a little pretentious - not Ed, or Eddie, but Edward.")

I couldn't believe I got it organized so quickly, but everything at the studio is done quickly. Below is what we planned to see at the studio. They were impressed; I hope you will be as well. [Note to self: why am I talking to myself like I'm talking to an audience? I need to schedule extra time with my shrink to figure this one out!]

Tour itinerary
1. Archives – First we will talk to the experts about the History of Essbase Studio.
2. Script Writing and Plot Development - It turns out we don't have the time or energy to go see how the design for an Essbase cube is done. If you are interested in this longer detour, you should read the Look Smarter Than You Are with Essbase: An Administrator's Guide.
3. Central Casting – we've got to get the players for our EPM box office hit. The databases and tables take center stage when working with Essbase Studio.
4. Talent Scouts – The schemers; or in our case the mini-schemas have all the connections and really decide who is used and how.
5. Wardrobe – This is where Dimension Members get fitted and dressed up with filters sorting and alterations
6. Set Design – We will take the Dimension members and create Hierarchies from them.
7. Dubbing – After we have our members and hierarchies defined, we need to add a voice to them by adding aliases.
8. Makeup – Once we have our hierarchies, we will make Cube Schemas and Essbase model out of them.
9. Distribution – We have our blockbuster ready, but we need to create our Essbase database and populate it, we do this by Deploying Cubes.
10. The Stunt Show – Once our Essbase database is in place, we can extend functionality by creating Drill through reports.
11. The Theme Park – We take a wild ride by exploring what is XOLAP and to implement it.
12. Animation – No good tour is complete until you see how application administration is done.

It figures this is a 12 step program. I should be used to those by now.

The tram arrived. Why it looked like a little yellow school bus I have no idea, but the seats were comfy and the champagne was chilled and ready. ER and Tracy were getting antsy and tired of listening to me already. It is time to get the tour going, so everyone into the limo – oh, okay; on the Essbase Studio tram.

Chapter 2:
The Archives

Tip!

This symbol will show up to give you good ideas and hints. For instance, the first tip is that if you find you don't like my humor or the way the book is written, you can skip the first paragraph of most chapters and not miss any important content!

The first stop of the Studio trolley is the Archives. Does anyone ever clean up in here? It was too much like the inside of my mind – dusty, dirty, cobwebbed, crazy, and full of useless facts.

Behind the crusted counter was a tolerably tall sort of scrawny gawking geek whose excruciating posts on Essbase essentials curiously contained goofy gaggles of weird words that had me hunting through wily ol' Webster's for definitions. I couldn't decide if his facile fluency was due to incredible intelligence or imbecilic idiocy. Cameron was his name; the only resemblance to the goddess Cameron Diaz started and ended with their moniker. When Cameron and Tracy shook hands, it was a true geek to geek moment. Why don't the dames fall for me this way? No matter, the puckish pedantic professor started to endlessly expound why the history of Essbase Studio was so important. Incredibly important to elongated egg-heads like him and Tracy, maybe, to me, not so much. But as Tracy stood raptly rooted to one spot listening to Essbase Studio's past, present, and future, I turned on my iTelephone's recorder so I could determinedly decode and document his predictive prognostications. My dusty dictionary and I would have a date with destiny trying to decipher the discourse.

It turns out Essbase Studio had humble beginnings. It started out in the dark ages of Arbor trees as two simple-minded options in Essbase: SQL Interface and SQL Drill Through. Both were "costed" options. You had to pay extra for them, and because of that, companies limited their usage of the products.

SQL Interface was implemented as part of load rules. While the most common method of getting data in early versions was from flat file, using the SQL interface you could write SQL code, embed it into the load rule, use an ODBC driver on the server and retrieve data for dimension building or data loading. For diehard purists, this method is still available today and in System 9 became a free option to the product. For simple retrieves it still works well. It works so well, Essbase Studio incorporates this functionality to do its retrievals (albeit in a much more eloquent way). Nevertheless SQL interface does the heavy lifting for Essbase Studio.

SQL Drill Through was destined to be a fate of the crewmember in the red shirt in Star Trek. You know the guy. He is the one who beams down with the Captain, Spock and Bones only to get quickly killed off. SQL Drill Through allowed you to define one or more reports from within Excel to bring back relational data based on the names of one or more dimension parameters. It was cumbersome to say the least. Each cube had to have its own drill through reports defined and they acted like some of the divas of today, temperamental and difficult to deal with. SQL Drill Through met its demise when version 6 came out. Some companies figured out how to use unsupported versions all the way through System 9. It was killed off because other, better ways to accomplish drill through to detail were coming.

The next product introduced by the handy Hyperion developers was Essbase Integration Server (EIS). About the time it was released, the Hyperion marketing department was bored and decided to rename products left and right. The product went through names quicker than Elizabeth Taylor went through husbands. It was (in no particular order):

EIS

       Essbase Integration Server and/or
       Essbase Integration Services and/or
       Enterprise Integration Server

HIS

       Hyperion Integration Services

AIS

       Analytic Integration Services

What exactly is EIS (the final name) and what does it allow you to do? EIS expands on both the SQL Interface and SQL Drill Through solutions. EIS allows you connect to an underlying relational repository (in most cases a star or snowflake schema) to create metadata structures to build cubes, populate them, and provide drill back capabilities to end-users. EIS runs as a service and the service acts as a conduit to do all of these tasks. This is a good thing and a bad thing. First, the good: EIS allows users to:

- Create models to designate the relationships (joins) between tables (a.k.a MetaModel).
- Define hierarchies associated with the model.
- Create a Metadata Outline to define the hierarchies for a cube and the associated properties

- Implement Hybrid Analysis cubes. These are cubes that store part of the data in Essbase and part of the data in the underlying relational source. To end-users Hybrid Analysis cubes provide an Essbase-like interface and analysis capabilities even though detailed information is stored relationally. A Hybrid Analysis cube allows a user to store data in an Essbase cube and, when it gets to a certain level, EIS issues SQL statements to get greater detail in a view that looks just like it is drilling deeper into a cube.
- Create Drill Through reports to get additional data from a relational source that is not normally available to a cube (e.g. "columns and columns type reports with text attribute information that is difficult to store in Essbase or invoice detail to summarized financials stored in Essbase).
- Automate the build and load process using CBS files.

The idea is to give developers a single interface to be able to build cubes more quickly from existing data warehouses. In a way it works. IT had thought of Essbase as a finance toy in the past, but having a relational interface seems to make them more apt to use the product. However, with the good comes the opportunity for improvement. Some of the challenges with EIS are:

- The service has to be running to deploy a cube and the service goes down frequently.
- Administrators find limitations in the ability to make updates to Essbase cubes (e.g. if you want to delete and re-add a dimension, you have to rebuild the entire Essbase cube).
- Drill through reports are designed and associated with a single metadata outline. If you want the same drill through report on multiple cubes, you have to recreate it multiple times.
- Drills through reports are hard to debug. If you have problems with a report, it can take a long time to figure out what is wrong with it.
- In order to assign a new drill through report to an Essbase cube, you have to perform an Outline update.
- Drill through is supported on data cells only (no members).
- EIS faces restrictions on member formulas.
- You are limited to relational sources for source data.

In Enterprise Performance Management Fusion Edition 11.1.0 (hereafter and forever known as Version 11) Essbase Studio was born. The idea was to take the good points from EIS, add functionality from Essbase Administration Services (EAS), and make them better. How did they do that, you ask? (If you didn't ask, then you aren't actually reading the words on this page.)

While there is a whole mini-series on the features of Essbase Studio, I will give you the trailers. You know, the short eye catching candy we see for coming attractions. Figure 1, courtesy of my friends at Oracle, shows some of the features and how they relate to the features of EIS. [Note to self: Figure 1 refers to a chart, not trying to figure out the number "one" or the figure of the young starlets hanging all over Edward because they think he is now a producer.]

Characteristic	*EIS*	*Studio*
Data Sources	Relational only (ODBC DSNs)	Relational (No need to pre-define ODBC DSN), Flat file, EPMA, OBIEE Data source exploration
Reusability	Very limited support (one model can have multiple Metaoutlines)	All logical elements (Logic Element, Hierarchy, Cube, DT report, etc)
Cube Load	Only streaming loads are supported through EIS (which are slower)	Two load options are supported (non-streaming thru Essbase SQL interface vs. streaming via Studio)
Lineage	Not supported	Supported
Drill Through – To	Relational/URL; tightly coupled with cube model	Relational/URL/OBIEE/FDM, Dynamic DTR Association
Drill Through – How?	Excel Add-in	Smart View
Drill Across	Not supported	From Smart View client jump from one cube to another (Future)

Language and API Interface	OLAPICMD (command console for batch load)	CPL, Maxl (for Cube deployment only), Java API (cpld). XML Import/Export
Security via Shared Services	Not supported	Supported
New Essbase Features (11.x)	Not supported	Supported – Varying Attributes, Smart List, Calendar Hierarchy, XOLAP, Text/Date Measures, Format Strings, etc
Essbase Load Optimization	Key/Alias optimization	Key/Alias optimization, ASO parallel Dataload, TPT API, OCI Chain Grouping (Dimbuild)
Catalog Migration	N.A.	EIS Catalog Migration
Hybrid Analysis	Available (HOLAP/ROLAP)	In XOLAP form
Deployment History	Not supported	Supported

Figure 1 - Enhancements from EIS to Studio*

*Supplied by the Oracle Essbase Studio Development team

These features and attractions are detailed in the rest of the book.

What will the sequel to Essbase Studio (unlike SQL) look like? According to a number of presentations that I've attended on the Hyperion Product Roadmap, the vision for Essbase Studio is to completely replace EIS and EAS as a single administrative console for the development and maintenance of Essbase cubes. If we follow the yellow brick roadmap for the product, we see it meeting and joining with some interesting characters along its path to the Emerald city.

Chapter 3:
Central Casting

"On your left is the street where we have filmed some of our more famous features. You remember 'How to Succeed in Planning Without Really Trying', 'One Flew Over the Spreadsheet', and the smash hit '0011001000110000001100000110001: A Space Odyssey'." The tour guide was trying to give some filler as we headed to central casting, but Edward was too busy trying to figure out who should play him to hear her. Through his mind raced ideas like Brad Pitt, Johnny Depp and Tom Cruise. Tracy was thinking about the same thing, but her ideas for an actor to play Edward were more like Jerry Lewis, Pee Wee Herman and Jonny 5. At any rate, it was too early to try to figure that out.

Since it was premature to actually work on their production, "The Dork who Juggled Wolverines", I told them we would follow the creation of another one of our blockbusters titled "TBC". While I left it to their imagination what that meant, I'll fill you in on the secret if you promise not to tell anyone. It stands for "The Beverage Company" and it is a remake of the most awesome adventure we have made called Sample.Basic!

OK, so why are we at central casting? Because this is where we can get connected. You have to have your sources and this department is really well connected. There are a ton of connections these people can make. What kind of connections?

- Delimited flat files
- Relational Tables
  - o Oracle
  - o SQL Server
  - o MYSQL
  - o DB2
  - o Teradata
  - o Netezza
- OBIEE
- EPMA
- Essbase (but currently only as the target of a deployment)

You can't connect to Excel files, but you could save the excel file as a .csv file and use the file that way!

Tip!

The first connection we have to make is to Studio itself.

"Oh boy, we actually get to do something besides listen to the boring tour guide!" Edward quipped. I could tell Edward was afflicted with a case of ADHD and got bored and distracted easily.

GETTING STARTED

First we need to connect to Essbase Studio itself.

1. From the start menu, select Oracle EPM System >> Essbase>> Essbase Studio>> Essbase Studio Console:

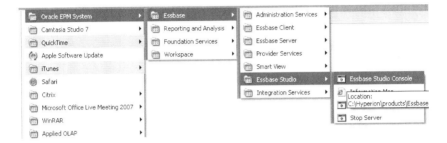

2. In the login dialog box enter your Studio Server location, User ID and Password and click OK:

Did you get an error? If so, check our list of "must do" tasks listed in the Foreword and Forewarned section at the beginning of this book. Did you remember to provision the ID to have access to Essbase Studio? Is the Studio Service Running?

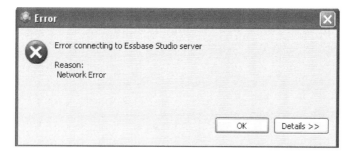

Tip!

Even if you are not provisioned properly, you may still be able to log in. You will not know you have a problem until you try to create a data source connection; then you will get a meaningless "Connection refused" error.

3. If everything worked properly, you should see the following screen:

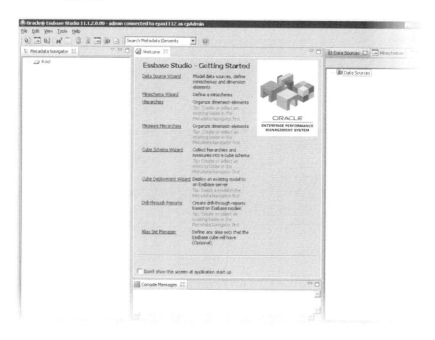

Now that we are connected, let's take a brief tour of the set (a tour within a tour, two tours for the price of one). The stage is designed for a three act play. Stage right (I'm left handed so I read from right to left), is where you define data sources and minischemas. ('What is a minischema?' you may ask 1) because you are reading and 2) because you probably don't know yet. Don't worry; we'll explain all of the terms for Essbase Studio in just a bit.). Just a word of warning, the picture below shows the 11.1.2.1 and earlier layout. In 11.1.2.2 the minischemas were moved to be within data sources (read about in in chapter 4)

Stage center is the real work area. It is used for visual representations. Notice the welcome screen with all sorts of wizards you can use to help you through the process. This area will change based on what you are doing. It will also create tabs to allow you to switch between different work areas and tasks.

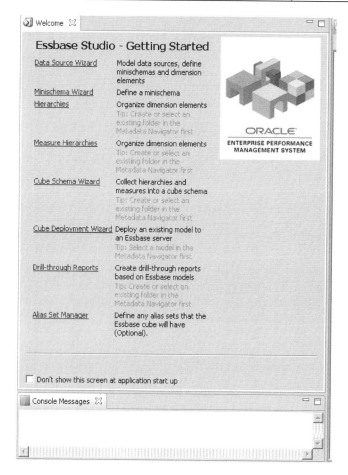

Stage Left is where you create your complete production from Wardrobe (creating metadata members and other elements) to Distribution (Cube Deployment). Your production will include:

- File structures
- Metadata members
- Hierarchies
- Cube schemas
- Drill Through reports

It looks pretty boring right now, but won't for long!

RECONNECTING TO STUDIO

If you spend a lot of idle time reading the book instead of actually performing the exercises or if you go to lunch, when you try to do something in Studio, you may get the following message:

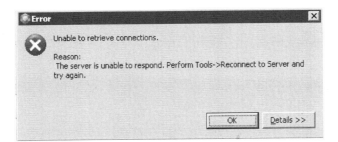

This means your session has timed out. Reconnecting to Studio is pretty simple and the message even tells you how to do it. Simply go to the Tools menu and select Reconnect to Server. Enter your password and you are good to go.

Tip!

The default timeout is set at 1 hour. You can change this in the server.properties file with the setting server.timeoutPeriod= X where X is the number of seconds.

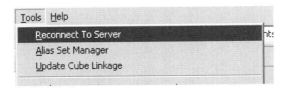

FLAT FILE CONNECTIONS

Let's get started by making a few connections of our own –specifically, to flat files. For us to connect to flat files, they must exist on the server under the directory specified in the server.properties file. It is possible and often advisable to create subdirectories within this main directory. In our case, we are going to look for the files in a directory called TBC_Samples. These files are created as part of the Studio install.

1. Right click on the Data Sources item in the right hand pane and select New>> Data Source:

2. The Connection Wizard Dialog appears. Give the Connection a name (we called ours "TBC_Flat_Files" and select "Text File" as the data source type:

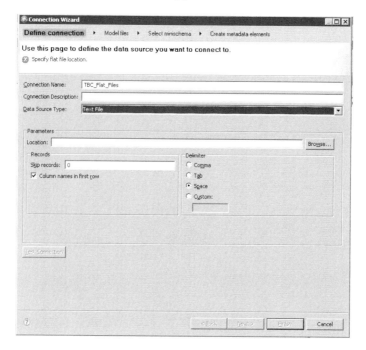

3. Click on Browse to find the file location:

4. Navigate to the TBC_Samples directory. If you click on the directory name the list of available files will appear in the right hand pane (provided that you installed the files properly). Click OK:

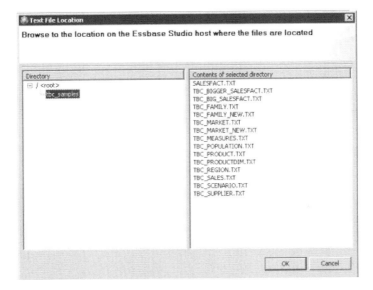

For flat files you can set default properties for the files that can be overridden later.

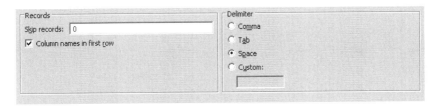

5. Click Next and you will get the list of files in the directory. This is where you can decide what files will be included in the Connection and the properties for each file (e.g.

SALESFACT.TXT with a space delimiter, headers set to true and skip rows set to 0).

Location: server123:///tbc_samples

Select all | Clear all | Filter: [   ] | 0 of 15 visible files selected (0 of 15 of all files selected)

☐ SALESFACT.TXT [delimiter: space; headers: true; skip rows: 0]
☐ TBC_BIGGER_SALESFACT.TXT [delimiter: space; headers: true; skip rows: 0]
☐ TBC_BIG_SALESFACT.TXT [delimiter: space; headers: true; skip rows: 0]
☐ TBC_FAMILY.TXT [delimiter: space; headers: true; skip rows: 0]
☐ TBC_FAMILY_NEW.TXT [delimiter: space; headers: true; skip rows: 0]
☐ TBC_MARKET.TXT [delimiter: space; headers: true; skip rows: 0]

6. Click on the name (not the checkbox) for TBC_Family.txt. You will see a sample of the data in the box below. Notice that it does not appear to be formatted correctly:

☐ SALESFACT.TXT [delimiter: tab; headers: true; skip rows: 0]
☐ TBC_BIGGER_SALESFACT.TXT [delimiter: tab; headers: true; skip rows: 0]
☐ TBC_BIG_SALESFACT.TXT [delimiter: tab; headers: true; skip rows: 0]
☐ **TBC_FAMILY.TXT [delimiter: tab; headers: true; skip rows: 0]**
☐ TBC_FAMILY_NEW.TXT [delimiter: tab; headers: true; skip rows: 0]
☐ TBC_MARKET.TXT [delimiter: tab; headers: true; skip rows: 0]

Records

Skip records: [0]

☑ Column names in first row

Delimiter

○ Comma
◉ Tab
○ Space
○ Custom:
[   ]

▥ FAMILYID,FAMILY,FAMILY_ALIAS,INTRODATE

1,100,Colas,1996-03-25 00:00:00.000
2,200,Root Beer,1995-09-27 00:00:00.000
3,300,Cream Soda,1996-06-26 00:00:00.000
4,400,Fruit Soda,1996-10-01 00:00:00.000

7. Change the delimiter from Tab to Comma. It should now look like this:

▥ FAMILYID	▥ FAMILY	▥ FAMILY_ALIAS	▥ INTRODATE
1	100	Colas	1996-03-25 00:00...
2	200	Root Beer	1995-09-27 00:00...
3	300	Cream Soda	1996-06-26 00:00...
4	400	Fruit Soda	1996-10-01 00:00...

8. See what happens if you uncheck "Column names in first row" and what happens if you change the skip records from 0 to 1 or 2.

9. Change the values back to 0 and re-check the checkbox.

What if your file doesn't have column headings? It would look pretty ugly if you just had the default of Col_0, Col_1. You can modify column headings by clicking the Edit Column Properties button and, column by column, changing the column name and/or its data type.

10. Click the Edit Column Properties button:

Notice you can change the column name and/or the data type:

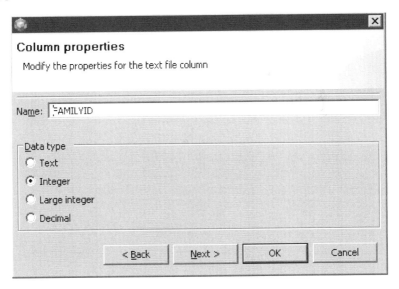

Now that you have changed the properties, let's make sure this is added to our connection.

11. Check the box next to the file name:

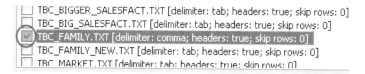

12. Repeat the procedure (change the delimiter, verify the column headings and data types, then checkmark the file to be included) for the files:
    - SALESFACT.TXT
    - TBC_MARKET.TXT
    - TBC_MEASURES.TXT
    - TBC_PRODUCTDIM.TXT
    - TBC_SCENARIO.TXT

Tip!

If you set a property wrong, to correct it, you have to delete the file from the data source and re-add it.

13. Click Finish.

You will see the data source connection is created with new flat file data sources. If you expand TBC_Flat_Files, you will see each of the individual flat files brought in as part of the source:

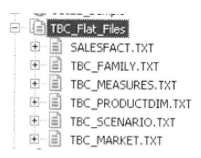

RELATIONAL CONNECTIONS

No, I'm not talking about nepotism here; although, my wife's nephew's third cousin is on the payroll earning lots of money as a good for nothing flunky - but I digress. I'm referring to getting data from a database like Oracle or SQL Server.

Tip!

New in version 11.1.2.2 is the ability to connect to Oracle RAC databases, being able to enter the nodes. (see picture below)

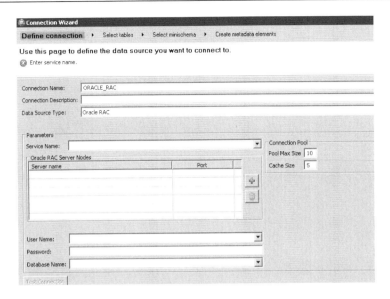

In my case, I have a SQL Server database called TBC_Sample that I am going to connect to; you will most likely need to use different connection properties to connect to your data source (e.g. Data Source Type, Server Name, Database Name, ID and Password).

1. Just like when creating the flat file data source, right click on Data Sources in the right pane and select New.

2. In the screen that appears, enter a Name for your data source (I like Fred, but typically people choose something more meaningful like TBC_Sample) and optionally a Description.

3. Fill in the relational connection information: Data Source Type (in my case Microsoft SQL Server), Server Name, Port, Relational database ID and Password, and Database Name.

4. You can press the Test Connection button to see if you have a connection (or you can be more creative and drop down the list of database names). If you have names, you know the connection worked without the silly connect button. In some databases you need to click the little fetch databases icon next to the database list:

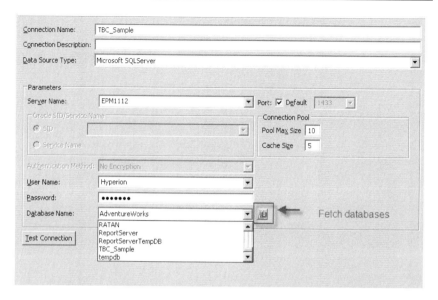

5. Click Next and you will get the list of tables in the database. Move the tables you need for your Essbase models from the left pane to the right pane.

6. For our the exercises in this book, make sure to select the tables - FAMILY, MARKET, MEASURES, POPULATION, PRODUCT, REGION, SALESFACT, SCENARIO and SUPPLIER:

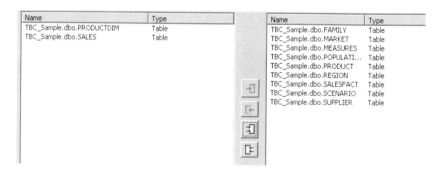

Notice the lock option. If you want to be selfish and prevent anyone from doing anything in Essbase Studio while you are looking at them, click the lock catalog during exploration. I always knew you didn't like to share!

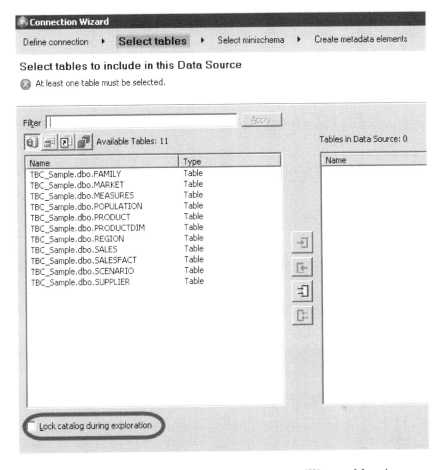

What's that you say? You have a gazillion tables in your database and it's hard to find the right one? Well, that is why we have the Filter Option. Enter your search criteria in the text box next to Filter (with wildcards, if necessary) and click Apply. Note, this is for example only. Since you already selected Product in a previous exercise, you will only see PRODUCTDIM in the list:

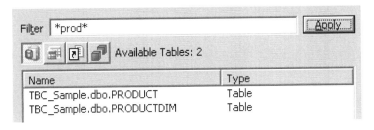

You are still not happy? You can't find what you want because you use views instead of tables. That is what these little icons do in the Essbase Studio:

They let you show or hide tables, views, aliases and synonyms respectively. One or more can be selected at a time.

7. Now that you have moved the tables over, click Next and you will see the following image for a period of time:

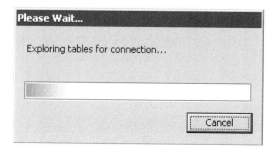

If you are bored right now and want to get a drink and some food, then you can click Finish and come back later. I have to go to the bathroom, so even though you are truly excited about moving on, click Finish anyway.

8. Click Finish (in case you missed the previous instruction).

You will see the data source connection is created with new relational table data sources. If you expand TBC_Sample, you will see each of the individual tables brought in as part of the source. If you expand on a specific table, you will see the columns within that table:

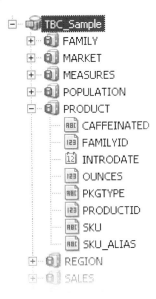

At this point we have both flat file and relational sources defined in Essbase Studio. If those are the only types of connections you need, you can skip to the Chapter 4: Talent Scouts (or the "Minischemas" chapter). Please continue reading to learn more about the other types of Essbase Studio sources like EPMA.

EPMA CONNECTIONS

Enterprise Performance Management Architect (EPMA) provides a single interface to build, deploy, and manage all financial applications for Planning, Financial Management, Essbase and Profitability and Cost Management. EPMA uses a visual interface to manage, link, and synchronize applications for Hyperion administrators.

EPMA contains the following components:

- Dimensions Library – one place to create and maintain dimensions across Hyperion applications
- Applications Library – one place to create and manage Hyperion applications
- Data Synchronization View – synchronize data across Hyperion applications
- Application Upgrade – upgrade Planning, FM and Essbase applications from previous releases
- Job Console – view a summary of Dimension Library and Application activities like imports, deployments and data synchronizations

So why do you care about integrating EPMA with Essbase Studio? If you are using EPMA's Dimensions Library as the central place for dimension maintenance, you will definitely want to integrate those dimensions into Essbase Studio and Essbase cubes deployed through Studio. In order to do so, you must create a connection to EPMA (as you can guess by now, to create an EPMA connection, you first have to have EPMA installed and configured).

The connection is very similar to other connections but to be visible to Studio, the dimensions in EPMA must in the shared library.

1. In Essbase Studio, right click on Data Sources and select New -> Data Source.
2. Enter a Connection Name for the data source and optional description.
3. Select Dimension Server as the Data Source Type.
4. Enter the server name where EPMA is installed along with the ID and password:

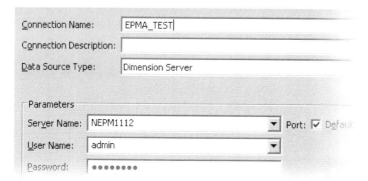

9.   Click Next.
10. Select the dimensions you want to include from EPMA and click Finish:

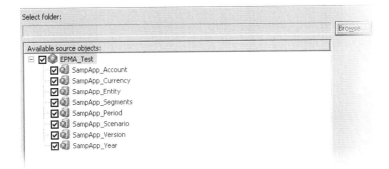

Now your EPMA dimensions are ready for modeling!

You cannot expand dimensions like you can with tables nor can you incrementally update them. You have to recreate the connection.

Tip!

OBIEE CONNECTIONS

While it would take a book in itself to describe all of the features and functionality of Oracle Business Intelligence Enterprise Edition (OBIEE), the compressed definition is: OBIEE is a complete business intelligence reporting solution with a myriad of data sources. It can provide you with formatted and ad-hoc reporting, dashboards and scorecards. Data sources, calculations, metrics and hierarchies are managed in a common enterprise data model. This makes it an ideal source for building Essbase cubes through Studio. The connection sequence to connect to OBIEE is similar to other connections.

1. In Essbase Studio, right click on Data Sources and select New -> Data Source.
2. Enter a Connection Name for the data source and optional description.
3. Select Oracle Business Intelligence as the Data Source Type.
4. Enter the server name where OBIEE is installed along with the ID, password and the database name (If you don't get a list of database names, there is something wrong with your connection):

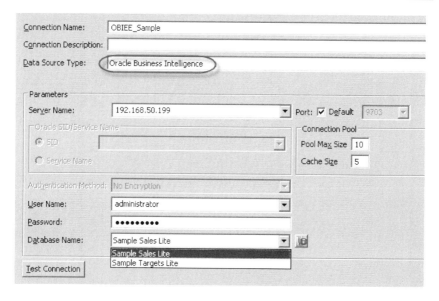

5. Click Next.
6. Select the Tables to include in the source.
7. Click Finish:

Now your OBIEE source is available to Essbase Studio.

CONNECTION MODIFICATIONS

It is hard to believe, but in the first version of Essbase Studio you could not make changes to a table or view definition within a connection once you created it (from now on I'll use the term table to refer to tables and views). In our ever-changing worlds of development, that made Studio a difficult product to implement. You had to constantly start over or create new connections or user defined tables. This limitation is removed in Version 11.1.2. With 11.1.2 Essbase Studio, you can update and modify the connections in a number of ways including:

• Adding columns to definitions

- Updating the data type of a column
- Removing Columns*
- Deleting tables*

*You may remove columns or delete tables only if the columns or tables are not being used in defined metadata elements (more on metadata elements in a few chapters).

Tip!

If you are working on the 11.1.1.X series, you have to delete the **entire** model going backward from Essbase model, hierarchies, Aliases, metadata members, minischemas and finally data source in order to make changes to table or view definitions.

ADDING TABLES\VIEWS TO A DATA SOURCE

Once you create your data source, it is possible to add tables or views to it at a later time. For example, we want to add a second fact table for use in a schema.

1. On the data source TBC_Sample, right click and select Incremental Update:

2. In the screen that appears, select the table "Sales" to add to our data source.
3. Use the right arrow to move it to the right pane:

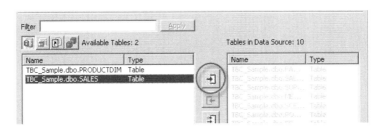

4. Click OK. The table/view will be added to your data source.

ADDING, MODIFYING AND DELETING COLUMNS

You can update your tables/views if they change. This can be done for a single table or for an entire data source. For this example I modified the Product table in my SQL Server instance, adding a column called CASE_QTY:

Column Name	Data Type	Allow Nulls
PRODUCTID	int	☐
FAMILYID	int	☑
SKU	varchar(15)	☑
SKU_ALIAS	varchar(25)	☑
CAFFEINATED	varchar(5)	☑
OUNCES	int	☑
PKGTYPE	varchar(15)	☑
INTRODATE	datetime	☑
CASE_QTY	int	☑

To update the data sources in Essbase Studio,
1. Right click on the Product table and select Refresh:

2. A dialog will appear to show you the changes. Either check Select All or put a check in the box for the table(s) you want to update:

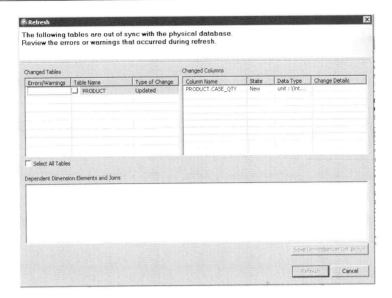

3. Click Refresh.
4. You will be notified if the change is successfully completed or if there are errors:

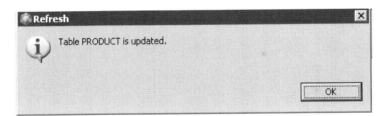

If you refresh the list of data sources in Essbase Studio, you can see the Product table was updated with the new column added:

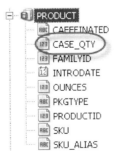

Follow the same procedure if you delete columns or if you update the data type of columns. See an example below when a column was removed from a table:

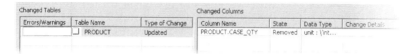

Changed Tables				Changed Columns			
Errors/Warnings	Table Name		Type of Change	Column Name	State	Data Type	Change Details
	PRODUCT		Updated	PRODUCT.CASE_QTY	Removed	unit : \'int…	

USER DEFINED TABLES

As I showed Edward and Tracy the data source connection process for Essbase Studio, Tracy appeared to be concerned. I skillfully ascertained the reason for her trepidation. It seemed the DBA required committee decisions for any changes to the database schema, so if she needed changes to the tables or view it would take an eternity to get approval and impact the release of her boffo blockbuster. I put her mind immediately at ease. We here at Essbase Studio have a solution for her called "User Defined Tables". I explained that, Tracy being the SQL guru she is, she could create a table within Essbase Studio based on her existing connection tables. This table is the equivalent of a view, since you can do the cool things like:

- Change column data types
- Join tables together
- Include subqueries
- Concatenate columns

Thinking I was trying to fool her, Tracy wanted a demo. I don't know why; she didn't know me well enough to know how much I lie. Though in this case, I was actually telling the truth, so it was easy to show her. You too can try this out (again, talking to imaginary people is not a good mental health sign).

1. Right click in the connection TBC_SAMPLE and select New
   >> User Defined Table:

2. In the dialog box that appears, select the TBC_Sample connection from the dropdown.
3. Enter the table name PRODUCT_FAMILY _CUSTOM.
4. Enter the following SQL statement as the Table Definition:

```
Select prod.*,fam.Family,fam.Family_Alias from
Product Prod
Join Family fam
on prod.familyid = fam.familyid
```

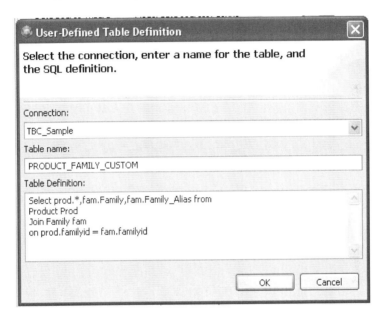

5. Click OK. You should see a new table added to your connection:

6. Right click on the table you just created and select show sample data. A table should appear with the table properties as you defined them:

PRODUCTID	FAMILYID	SKU	SKU_ALIAS	CAFFEINATED	OUNCES	PKGTYPE	INTRODATE	
1	1	100-10	Cola	TRUE	12	Can	Mon Mar 25 00:	
2	2	100-20	Diet Cola	TRUE	12	Can	Mon Apr 01 00:	
3	3	100-30	Caffeine Free C...	FALSE	16	Bottle	Mon Apr 01 00:	
4	4	200-10	Old Fashioned	TRUE	12	Bottle	Wed Sep 27 00:	
5	5	200-20	Diet Root Beer	TRUE	16	Bottle	Fri Jul 26 00:00	
6	6	200-30	Sasparilla	FALSE	12	Bottle	Tue Dec 10 00:	
7	7	200-40	Birch Beer	FALSE	16	Bottle	Tue Dec 10 00:	
8	8	300-10	Dark Cream	TRUE	20	Bottle	Wed Jun 26 00:	
9	9	300-20	Vanilla Cream	TRUE	20	Bottle	Wed Jun 26 00:	
10	10	300-30	Diet Cream	TRUE	12	Can	Wed Jun 26 00:	
11	11	400-10	Grape	FALSE	32	Bottle	Tue Oct 01 00:	
12	12	400-20	Orange	FALSE	32	Bottle	Tue Oct 01 00:	
13		400-30	Strawberry	FALSE	32	Bottle	Tue Oct 01 00:	

7. Now right click on the PRODUCT_FAMILY_CUSTOM table and select Properties.

8. Navigate through the properties of your custom table.

Clicking through the tabs, you can see how the columns are defined and the SQL used to create them. Can you change the columns or the SQL? No. Once a User defined table has been created, the only way to modify it is to delete it and recreate it. This can be done as long as it is not being used anywhere. To find out where it is being used, you could skip to the section on Lineage in Chapter 12: Studio Operations.

9. Repeat the steps adding a table named Sales_Ranking using the following SQL:

```
Select
1 as TABLE_ID,
'Poor' as TABLE_VALUE
Union
Select
2 as TABLE_ID,
'Average' as TABLE_VALUE
Union
Select
3 as TABLE_ID,
'Good' as TABLE_VALUE
```

Note: This is the Syntax for Microsoft SQL Server. For Oracle relational databases, you might need to add a "from Dual" to each select; for other relational sources, you are on your own.

Now that you understand the steps to create and modify data source connections for Essbase Studio, the casting process is complete. We've identified the main sources of data and we're now ready to join these sources together in preparation for Essbase modeling. Who better to aid us in this process but our Talent Scouts (a.k.a Minischemas).

Chapter 4:
Talent Scouts

As we entered the offices of the talent scouts, Edward was amazed at the group in the room. None of them was over 4 foot tall. I explained to Edward and Tracy the role of our talent scouts. They are the mini-schemers in the company - the guys that know all the members and their joins. Edward perked up at that statement, so I had to say it again – "JOINS" - (there is not a T in there, Edward!). Our talent scouts go out and create the minischemas. A minischema is the logical representation of the relationships between tables and within tables within a connection. It is important to know that minischemas are tied to data sources, you do not mix tables from multiple sources in a minischema. This fact is so important that in 11.1.2.2, minischemas were moved from their own tab in the Data Source Navigator to be part of the connection info.

In Studio we use two types of joins; joins between tables and joins within tables. The latter are called self joins or recursive joins and are used on tables that are arranged in Parent/child relationships. We also have two ways to create the joins; first, by introspection, and, second, manually. It should be noted that the creation of minischemas can be done as a continuous part of the data source build. After defining the data source, click Next instead of Finish and the wizard will walk you through the creation of the minischema (with or without introspection).

INTROSPECTION

Just like talent scouts discover new talent, a minischema uses introspection to discover joins between underlying relational sources (Tracy said she did yoga that allowed her introspection). In a way, Studio does something similar. It looks at all of the tables within a data source and, based on primary and foreign keys, figures out how the tables are related to each other. Of course, introspection only works for relational tables, and it works well if you have keys defined and not so well when you don't.

1. In the Essbase Studio, right click on the data source TBC_Sample and select Introspect:

2. Select "Create a new schema diagram" (and, if you want, change the name of the schema; we called ours TBC_SampleSchema).
3. Click Next:

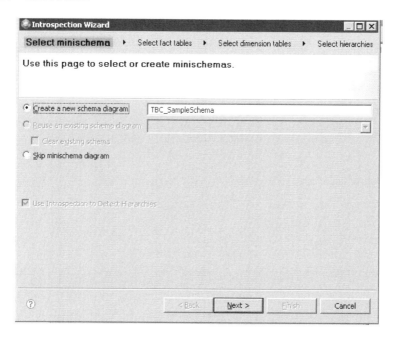

At the next screen, you will select the fact table. A fact table is usually the main table that stores the data values to be loaded to your Essbase model. It usually contains columns for your "facts" or data values and columns with foreign keys to the dimension tables (see our TBC_Sample SALESFACT table with fact columns highlighted):

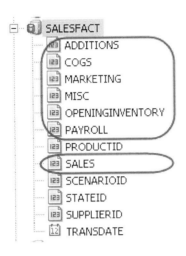

The wizard gives you the possibilities based on table attributes. For TBC_Sample data source, our fact table is SALESFACT:

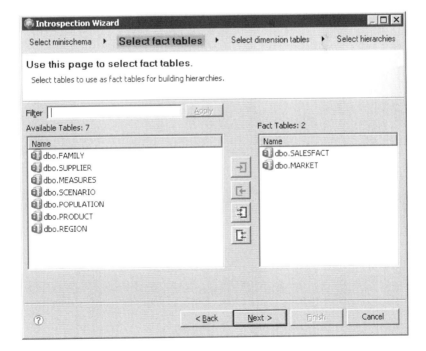

4. Since the fact table is indeed SALESFACT, remove MARKET from the Fact tables selected list by clicking on Market and using the left arrow:

5. Click Next.

At the next screen, you will select the dimension tables. A dimension table is usually the set of tables that stores the hierarchies and attributes about the dimension of data. The dimension tables will join to the main fact table based on a primary key or unique value defined for the table. Facts are rarely stored in dimension tables. The wizard gives you the possibilities based on table attributes.

6. In the Dimension table section of the Introspection wizard, select the following dimension tables – SCENARIO, PRODUCT, MARKET, FAMILY, POPULATION, REGION, MEASURES:

Tip!

Sometimes the tables will already be selected. If so, you have less work to do.

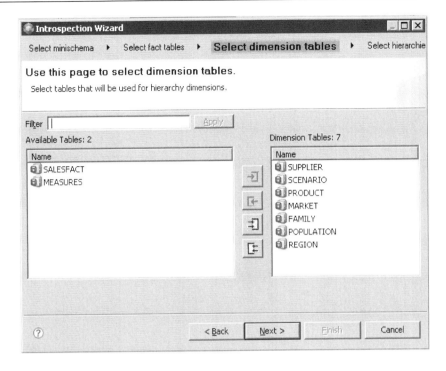

7. Click Next.

At the next screen, you can view the hierarchies that introspection was able to create. Note how the Introspection wizard built the hierarchies for us for the Product and Market dimension tables:

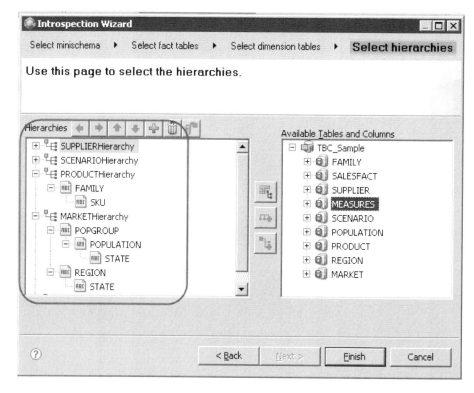

8. Review the hierarchies created by the Introspection Wizard.

If the wizard did not create some desired hierarchies, it is possible to manually create them, using the top icon in the middle of the screen. You can create a hierarchy, add a sibling to a hierarchy or add a child to a hierarchy:

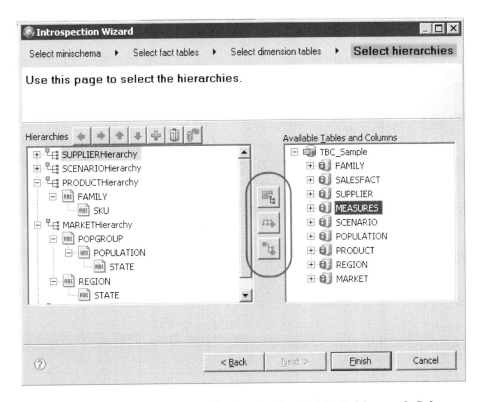

9. Select the Measures table in the Available Tables and Columns panel on the right portion of the wizard.
10. Click the top button to Add a Hierarchy. The Measures hierarchy should be created as an empty hierarchy.
11. With the new Measures hierarchy still selected, select the column "PARENT" in the Measures table under Available Tables and Columns.
12. Select the Add Column as Child button:

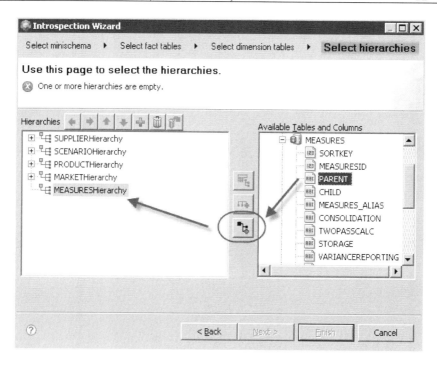

Parent should now reside under the MeasuresHierarchy:

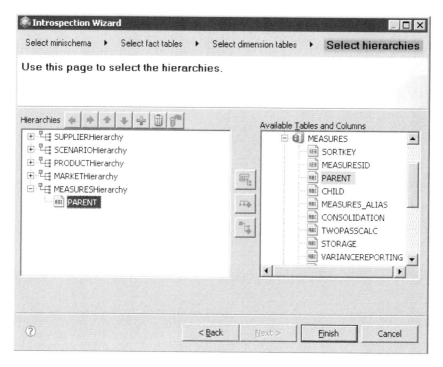

13. With the new Measures hierarchy, PARENT column selected, select the column "CHILD" in the Measures table under Available Tables and Columns.

14. Select the Add Column as Child button:

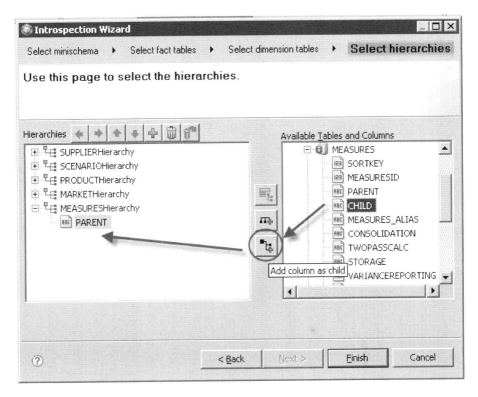

The resulting Measures hierarchy should look as follows:

You can use the buttons above the hierarchies to reorder the hierarchies or members in the hierarchies, to make a member a child, parent or sibling, or to delete an item:

15. Click Finish to complete the Introspection Wizard.

The minischema has been saved and a visual representation is shown in the working pane:

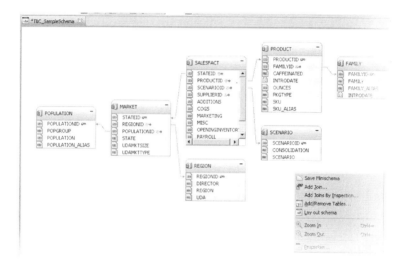

16. Right click in the pane and select Save Minischema. This allows it to show up on the Minischema tab or in the Data Source Navigator for 11.1.2.2:

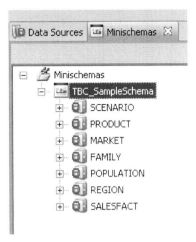

11.1.X layout

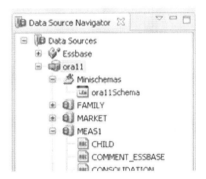

11.1.2.2 layout

A side effect of using introspection is that members and hierarchies are created in the metadata navigator in a folder for the data source:

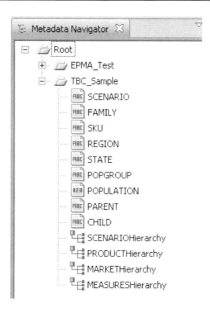

As a trailer for Chapter 5: Wardrobe, below you can see how the artifacts got added to the navigator. In that chapter we will introduce the Metadata Navigator and discuss how to add order to all of the metadata elements used for Essbase modeling.

MANUAL MINISCHEMAS

When we last left our Dynamic Duo they completed the task of introspection. Now, they were ready to delve into the unknown dark, gloomy world of the manual minischemas. (Say - I need to remember this; it sounds like a good plot for a movie.) I was ready to show Tracy and Edward – wait, where is Edward? After scouting about the room a bit, I found him mingling with the talent scouts; given his size he fit right in. Where was I... ah yes, I was talking about creating manual minischemas. Remember a minischema shows the relationships between tables and within tables. If you don't use introspection, you can create a manual minischema easily. "Why do I have to manually create a minischema?" Tracy asked. The response gushed forth from me as if I actually knew the answer.

In many cases you will be dealing with tables and views that are still in development and do not have indexes created, so you can't use introspection. There are a number of other reasons you will not be able to use introspection, including a need to make recursive joins or joins that are not intuitive. Fear not, for Studio gives you the ability to manually create joins.

Creating a Manual Minischema

To create a minischema manually,

1. From the Data sources right click on TBC_Sample and select New>>Minischema:

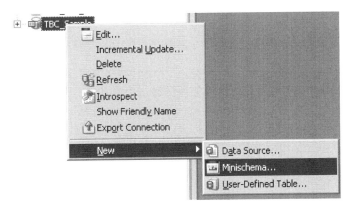

2. Name the schema (we called ours TBC_SampleManual_Schema) and, if you want, give it a description:

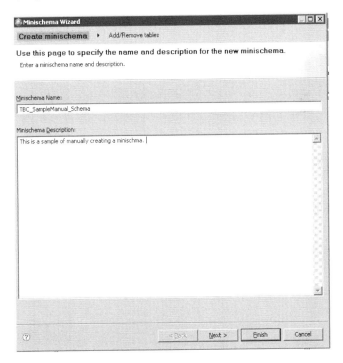

3. Click Next.
4. In the Connection select TBC_Sample

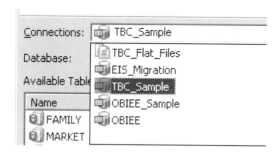

5. Select the tables you want included in the minischema and move them to the right hand pane using the arrow keys; for this exercises choose FAMILY, MARKET, MEASURES, POPULATION, PRODUCT, REGION, SALES, SCENARIO, and SUPPLIER:

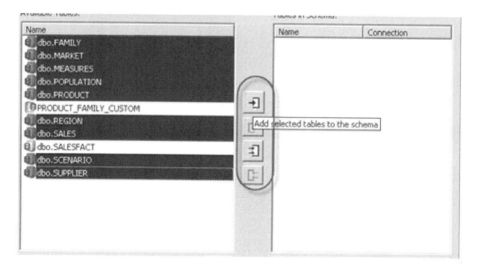

6. Click Next.

The Minischema will be created and a visual representation will be displayed in the working panel:

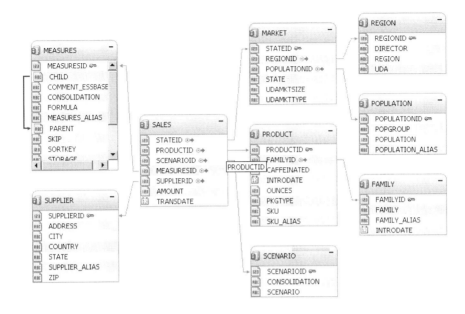

Tip!

As mentioned in the section on creating Flat file data sources, the only joins you can do on flat files are recursive joins.

Since the underlying relational repository had primary and foreign key relationships defined, Essbase automatically figured out most of the joins. If keys have not been defined for a relational source, you have to define the joins manually in Essbase Studio.

Creating a Manual Join

We have such a case for our exercises. Essbase Studio was unable to create one of the required joins. It did not understand that the Measures table uses a parent child relationship and did not create the recursive join. So now it is up to me.

To add a manual join in an Essbase Studio minischema,

1. Make sure you are in the visual diagram of the correct minischema within Studio (or on the desired minischema tab); e.g. TBC_SampleManual_Schema.

2. Right click on the column Child in the Measures table. Select Add Join:

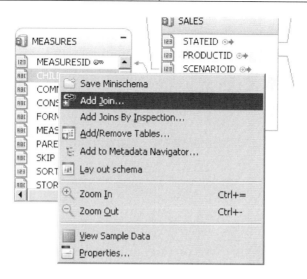

3. In the dialog that appears, select the Measures table to join to (a self-join) and select Parent as the column to join to. This is actually a dropdown box. If you click on it, you will get the list of columns. You can join on multiple columns with left, right or full outer joins:

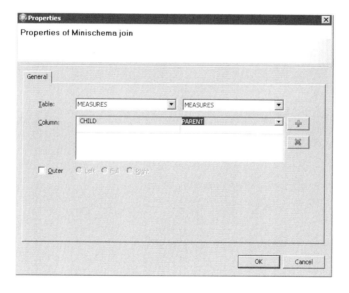

4. Click OK and you will see the recursive join has been added to the minischema visual diagram:

Tip!

It is also possible to make the joins by clicking on the member, holding down the left mouse key and dragging to the member you want to join to. This works well in most models, but large models may scroll as you try to do this, making it difficult.

Once the minischema has been created or if you make changes to it, remember to save it.

5. Right click in the working pane and select Save Minischema.

MODIFYING MINISCHEMAS

There are a number of things you can do to a minischema after it has been created: you can add or remove tables, reorganize the visual display or color code tables for visual clues.

There are two ways to add tables to a minischema. First, you can drag and drop them. Second, you can edit the minischema properties. Because I'm a nice guy (and I get paid by the word), I'll show you both methods.

Adding Tables to a Minischema by Drag and Drop

Make sure you have the Data source tab and not the minischema tab open and that it is expanded to the desired database. Select the table to drag it to the visual minischema display. You try it!

1. Select the Supplier table for the TBC_Sample data source.
2. Hold the left mouse key down and drag it onto the minischema in the work pane.
3. Once in the work pane, let go of the mouse key. Simple, isn't it?

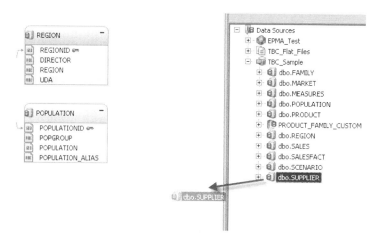

Depending on whether or not keys of the tables have been defined in the underlying relational repository, you may need to manually create the join(s) between this and other tables.

4. Save the minischema.

Adding Tables to a Minischema via Minischema Properties

1. Select the minischema tab and right click on the minischema to modify. Select Minischema Properties:

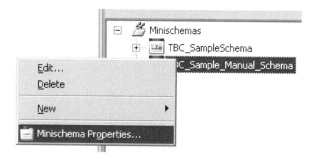

2. In the dialog that appears, click on the Add/Remove Tables tab.
3. Click on the Supplier table and use the right arrow to move it to the Tables in Schema:

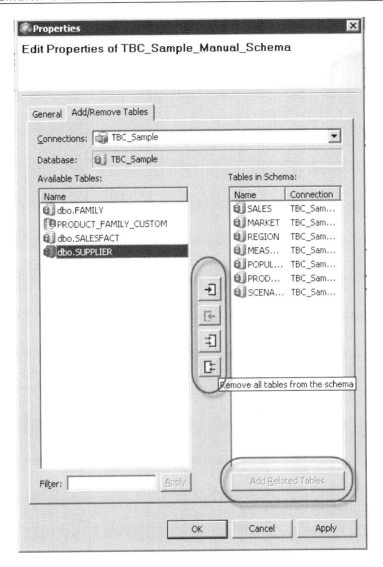

You can add or remove multiple tables at once using this method. Also notice the Add Related Tables button. If your tables are indexed, this button will add all tables that are associated to this table.

4. Click OK (to apply and exit the window) or Apply (to apply the changes but keep the window open).

5. Right click in the working pane and select Save Minischema:

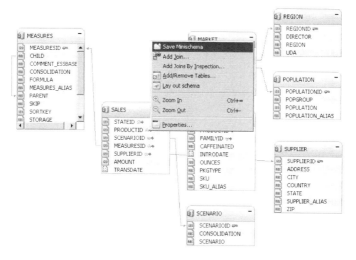

Organizing your Minischema

When you add tables and joins to a minischema, it is very easy to get a minischema display that is difficult to read (sort of like this book where lines cross all over the place). To make your minischema easier to read, format it! The process is so simple, in fact, that I won't use a numbered list to tell you how to do it. Right click on the minischema and select Lay out schema. That's it! Once you're done, your schema will be easier to read:

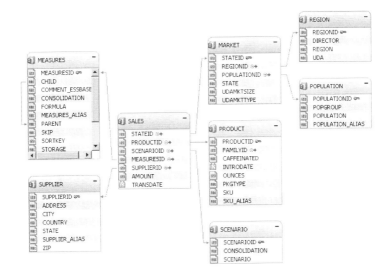

Color-coding your Minischema

Next we want to make it easier to identify key tables, like our fact table and the table we will use for Drill-through. Unless you are my son, who is colorblind, the following steps will show you how to provide visual clues about the tables in your minischema.

1. Select the Sales Table and right click.
2. Select Color >> Red (I like red; it stands out and is oh-so-pretty):

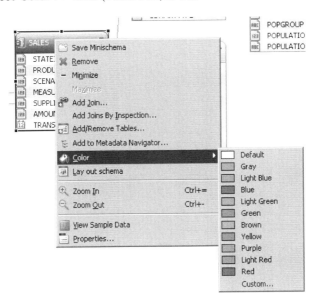

3. Select the Suppliers Table and make it green (we plan to drill through to this table in a later chapter):

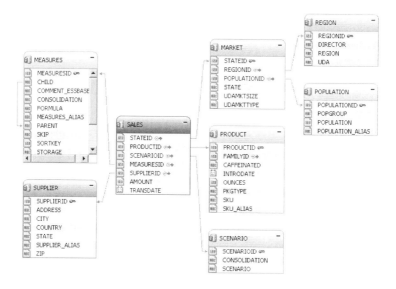

Isn't it much easier to see the important tables in the image? Well if you are only reading this book and not following along with the exercises, you won't see the pretty colors until you do it for yourself (since the book is printed in grey scale vs. color).

Create Data Sources and Minischemas in One Wizard

It was a dark and stormy afternoon when Tracy asked me why there was not an easier way to create the data source and minischema. She was ahead of me in every move.

"Remember that bathroom break when I was creating the data source and we clicked Finish?" I asked her.

Of course she remembered - she had had three bottles of water right before that (If you don't remember, look back to the end of Relational connections in Chapter 3). Had we clicked Next instead of Finish, we could have continued on with creating the minischema and more via the Wizard. So for fun, let's do that.

Before we get started back with the Studio Connection wizard, let's delete some of the elements we've created so far: any elements that may display in the Metadata Navigator, any minischemas and data connections related to the relational source TBC_Sample.

1. First to start over and give ourselves some practice, look at the Metadata Navigator (left panel) and see if a TBC_Sample folder exists. If it does, delete it by right clicking on it and selecting Delete :

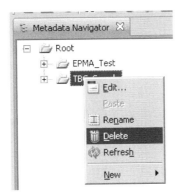

Tip!

If you created a EPMA connection, it automatically creates the Metadata members for the connection.

2. Now look at the right pane under minischemas and delete TBC_SampleSchema the same way. If the TBC_Samples_Manual_Schema exists delete it as well.
3. Switch to the Data Sources and delete the TBC_Samples connection the same way.

Now that you have a "clean" Essbase Studio environment, we're going to recreate the TBC_Sample connection but this time we're going to continue through the Connection Wizard to define data sources, minischemas, and metadata elements (we won't click Finish after the data source definition).

4. Right click on Data Sources in the right pane and select New.
5. In the screen that appears, enter a Name for your data source (remember I liked Fred, but got over ruled and used something more meaningful TBC_Sample).
6. Fill in the relational connection information: Data Source Type (in my case Microsoft SQL Server), Server Name, Port, Relational database ID and Password, and Database Name:

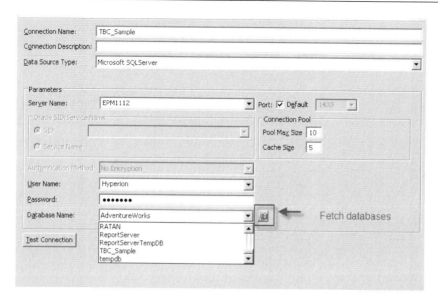

7. Click Next and you will get the list of tables in the database. Move the tables you need for your Essbase models from the left pane to the right pane.

8. For our the exercises in this book, make sure to select the tables - FAMILY, MARKET, MEASURES, POPULATION, PRODUCT, REGION, SALES, SCENARIO and SUPPLIER:

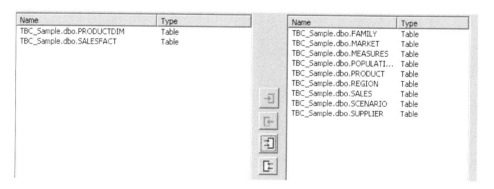

9. Click Next.

10. On the 'Select Minischema' screen that appears, click Create a new schema diagram radio button. Enter a name TBC_SampleSchema:

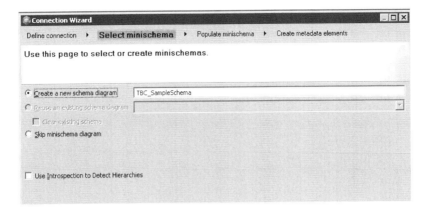

11. Click Next.

The following 'Populate minischema' screen appears, asking you which tables should be included in the minischema. By default all tables are selected but you could remove tables if not needed:

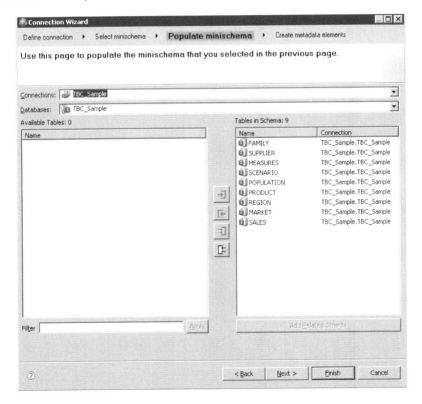

12. Click Next.
13. On the 'Create metadata elements' screen, click Browse:

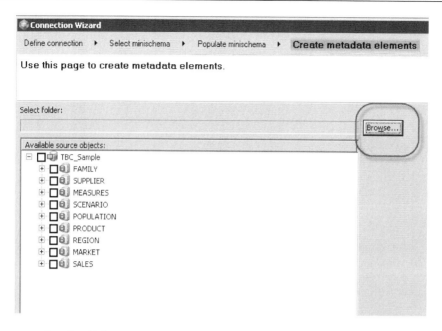

14. On the Select Folder screen, click the Create Folder button:

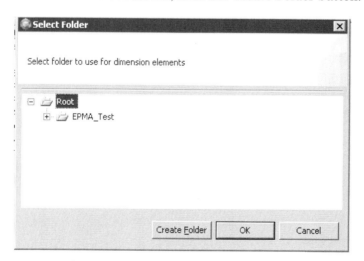

15. Give the folder the name TBC_Sample:

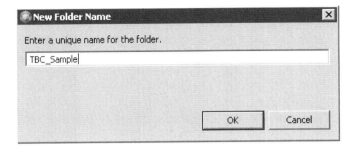

16. Click OK.
17. Click OK on the Select Folder Screen.
18. Expand the Family table under Available Data Sources and check the Family column:

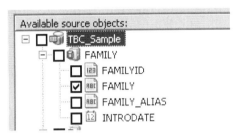

19. Repeat the previous step, choosing the following columns for the specified:

Table	Column to Check
Measures	Parent
	Child
Scenario	Scenario
Population	Population
Product	SKU
	Ounces
	PkgType
	IntroDate
Region	Region
Market	State
Sales	Amount

20. Click Finish. You will notice the Data Connections, Minischema and Metadata Navigator are populated:

21. You will need to add the self-join to the Measures table as described above in the section on creating Manual joins.

22. Go back to page 32 and add the Sales_Ranking table Add the members to the Dimension elements.

23. Finally save the minischema.

Tracy is now wondering who this mysterious Metadata Navigator is and what role does he play in Essbase cube building? This Essbase Studio tram tour just keeps getting more and more exciting for her and she's ready for the next stop. But wait, where is Edward? Of course, I found him still mingling with the talent scouts. I pulled him away and we're off to learn more about the Wardrobe department where we mix and match metadata elements to create cubes in style.

Chapter 5:
Wardrobe

It was a short tram ride to Wardrobe. Edward wanted to try on everything. He was especially intrigued by the Jedi Master's robe, so we let him have it. Somehow it worked with his nerdy-ness.

Why were we in wardrobe? Well, we had our cast of players (Data Connections) and we knew how they were going to interact and connect (Minischemas), but we had to get them set for what they would ultimately look like. From the data connections we saw the tables had many columns, but only a small number of them are really the actors in our production. We need to define who those members are and outfit them to be useful in production. This is where Dimension Elements come into effect. I think of a Dimension Element as an actor that will have a speaking part in our story. These actors are what ultimately make up our hierarchies, members and our Essbase model. For example, let's look at the Measures dimension table in our minischema. It has 14 columns including sort order, consolidation operators, parent, child, Aliases, formulas, etc.

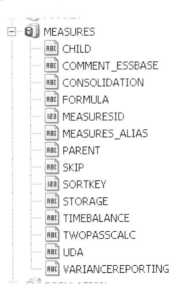

Of all of those 14 columns only two of them - Parent and Child - are needed to make up the hierarchy. The other columns are used to dress these measures. The dressing might be to sort them or set their consolidation.

Dimensional elements are part of a larger family of objects in Essbase Studio called Metadata elements. Dimensional elements will be used in other Metadata Elements like Hierarchies, Cube Schemas, Essbase models and Drill Through reports. We'll get to these other Metadata elements through the course of this book. For now, let's focus on the first step of creating the dimensional elements. Before you jump off the tram to start creating dimensional elements, we'll cover the instructional portion first.

There are four types of Dimension Elements:

- Columns from Tables
- Derived Text Members
- Text Lists
- Hard Coded Members

Columns from Tables

The easiest dimensional elements to understand are columns from tables. A column can provide a list of the members to build in a hierarchy. It is possible to modify these column values using functions and operators as well as filter and sort them (we will talk about sorting and filtering later in this chapter). For example, the State column in the Region table will be used to build the state members in the Essbase outline:

STATEID	REGIONID	STATE	UDAMKTSIZE
1	1	New York	Major Market
2	1	Massachusetts	Major Market
3	1	Florida	Major Market
4	1	Connecticut	Small Market
5	1	New Hampshire	Small Market
6	2	California	Major Market
7	2	Oregon	Small Market
8	2	Washington	Small Market
9	2	Utah	Small Market

For my purposes, Data Elements fall into this category even though the documentation separates them out. More on Data Elements in a later section.

Derived Text Members

Derived Text Members are members whose values are defined by a rule which references a numeric value, and whose values are defined by ranges. For example, a measure called Inventory Level could be derived off of Ending Inventory with values High, Medium and Low. These would be based on where the Ending Inventory data value ends up fitting.

Tip!

Derived text measures are not supported in XOLAP cubes.

Text Lists

Beginning in Essbase version 11, Essbase can store text and date information (which is just freaking awesome). Prior to 11, Essbase was limited to storing only numeric information in the data cells of a cube. This newer feature is called Text Lists provides the ability to perform analysis on text and dates in both ASO and BSO databases as you can see in Sample application below where we have a Text List for Package Type:

	Sales	Package Type
Cola	40013.2	Bottle
Diet Cola	12640.6	Can
Caffeine Free Cola	6281.6	Can
Colas	58935.4	Bottle
		Can
		Invalid

I remind Edward that they have Text Lists in their Juggling Wolverine cube for Customer Satisfaction Ratings:

Text List Manager   Modifications

Edit Mappings

	Name	ID
	Missing Name	#Missing
	Out Of Range Name	#OutOfRange
	Best Juggling in the World	1
	Mildly Entertaining	2
	Rather Eat Dog Food	3

Text List dimensional elements in Essbase Studio are used to create Essbase Text Lists. To create the Text Lists in Studio, both the text values and their associated numeric values have to be predefined in your relational source as separate columns. Studio connects to those sources and dynamically builds and updates the Text Lists along with loading data to an Essbase cube.

Hard Coded Members

Though it is not specifically spelled out in the documentation, you can create "hard coded members" or members that you manually define in Studio. These members do not reference an underlying data source column. When you create a member within a Hierarchy, Studio automatically creates a Dimension Element to support it. An example if this would be a member in the Scenario dimension named Variance. The Variance member does not exist in the source data, but will be needed in the hierarchy with its associated formula.

ORGANIZING THE METADATA NAVIGATOR

Before we start working on Dimension Elements, we should first talk about the organization of dimensional elements (and Metadata Elements) via the Metadata Navigator. The Metadata Navigator is the left panel of your Essbase Studio and is the place where you can organize all of the elements into folders and subfolders:

It is much easier to define the folder structure in the Metadata Navigator in the beginning versus trying to retrofit changes into the folder structures later.

When you log into Essbase Studio for the first time, the Metadata Navigator is empty. Remember the Connection Wizard where we defined the data source, created a minischema and created metadata elements (last section in the previous chapter)?

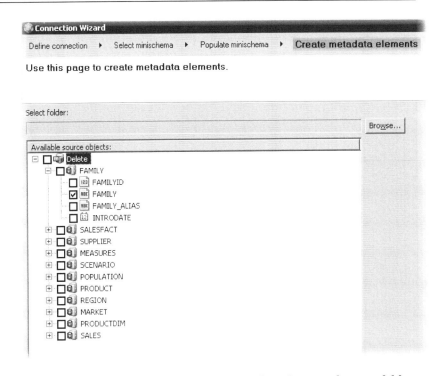

This last step in the Connection Wizard created some folders and dimensional elements in the Metadata Navigator:

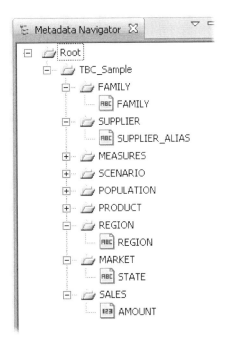

This is very similar to the way I like to organize my Metadata Navigator, though I have a few modifications and additions. It is far easier to set up the Metadata Navigator with standards now at the beginning of development than to go back later and try to organize it. In general, I organize my navigator to have four folders under a data connection: Members, Hierarchies, Cube Schemas and Drill through Reports:

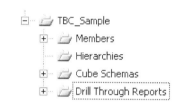

Within the Members folder, I keep all of the columns that are used to create hierarchies. I keep them separated by what table they are from, the way the wizard does. It is much easier to find defined dimension elements this way, especially if you have two columns with the same names. When might this occur? Think about it; if all of your tables are recursive (Parent/Child), every table could have a column called Parent and a column called Child. If these columns are all in a flat list, it is difficult to figure out which one is from what table. By organizing the Metadata Navigator by source table name, it is easier to find a specific column. By organizing the Metadata Navigator by metadata element type, I know where to look for hierarchies, cube schemas or drill through reports.

Please note that this is just my convention; there is nothing that says you can't do something different. I just found it works for me. I am the author so I do get to dictate what we'll do for these exercises. Follow along with me and let's build folders for organizing our TBC_Sample artifacts in the Metadata Navigator.

1. In the Essbase Studio, take a look at your Metadata Navigator tab on the left side of the Studio interface.

You will notice in my diagram (above) I have a TBC_Sample folder under another TBC_Sample Folder.

2. Right click on the child folder and select Rename:

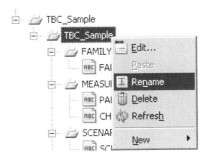

3. Change the name to Members (or to Dimension Elements as Studio calls them that, but I like Members more, rebel that I am) and hit Enter:

4. Right click on TBC_Sample and select New>>Folder:

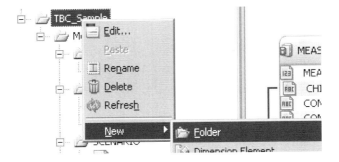

5. Name the Folder Hierarchies and click OK:

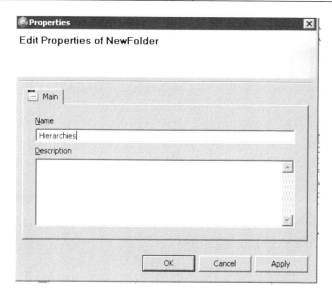

6. Repeat the steps to create folders for Cube Schemas and Drill Through Reports.

In the end, if you did your structure the way I did, you should have something that looks like:

Tip!

You can drag and drop artifacts between folders, but you cannot move folders themselves. It is easier to get the folder arrangement correct the first time than to try to move things around.

ADDING NEW DIMENSIONAL ELEMENTS

"Let's start with the easy things," I suggested to Edward and Tracy. I'm an easy kind of guy. First, when setting up your Metadata Elements, it is easy to forget something; for example, you need a column to use for an attribute of a dimension. In my case, I missed adding the

Caffeinated column during the Connection Wizard and I'll need this for the product dimension. There is an easy remedy for this; you can manually add columns from your minischemas to the Metadata Navigator at any time (you don't have to use the Connection Wizard).

1. From either the TBC_SampleSchema or TBC_Sample data source, expand the Product table, select the Caffeinated column, hold down the left mouse key and drag it over to the members in the metadata navigator (preferably into the Product sub folder):

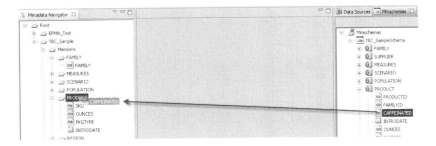

Wasn't that easy? You now have a Caffeinated column ready to use in the Navigator. In the same way, if I miss columns for an entire table, I drag the table over and delete the columns I don't need. For practice, let's do just that.

2. If a folder for Suppliers exists in the Dimension elements (right click on it and delete it. (depending on which exercises you did, it might or might not exist)

3. Drag the table Suppliers from the minischema to the members in the Metadata navigator:

4. Highlight SupplierID, Address, Supplier Alias and Zip, right click and select Delete. Those columns will be removed:

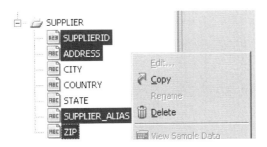

5. Since we really don't need the columns from the Supplier table, right click on the Supplier folder in the Metadata Navigator and select Delete. The folder and remaining columns will be removed.

MODIFYING DIMENSION ELEMENTS

In many cases, the data we get from our relational databases needs to be modified to fit our needs. These modifications could involve filtering members for certain criteria or sorting them for a specific order. Essbase Studio provides a number of functions and operators for modifying dimensional elements. The functions include Date, String and Numeric functions. The operators include Grouping, Logical, Mathematical and String operators. For example, our design calls for an alternate rollup of diet products but we do not have a column in the source table to give us those SKUs that are "diet". We can create our own dimensional element based on the SKU column and filter it to meet our needs. The filter will be based on the column SKU Alias and will filter values that contain the word "Diet".

1. In the Metadata Navigator right click on the sub folder Product (under TBC_Sample) and select New>> Dimension Element:

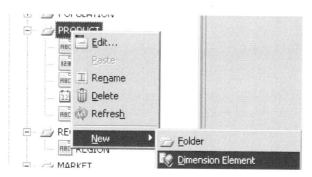

2. In the dialog that appears, enter Diet_SKUs as the name.
3. Expand TBC_Sample and Product and select SKU
4. Move the SKU dimensional element into the Caption Binding by either pressing the right Arrow or double clicking on SKU:

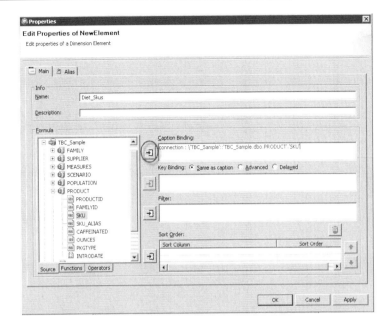

5. Next, to explore what functions we have available to us, click on the tab Functions located at the bottom left portion of the screen:

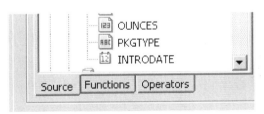

6. Expand the Functions to see we have a variety of functions we can use (date, string, and numeric):

Tip!

Flat file data sources only support the substr (substring) and || (concatenation) functions.

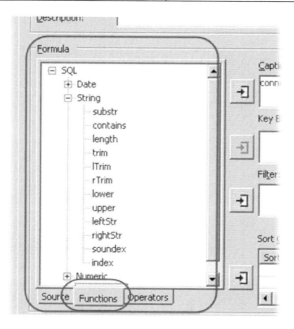

7. Select the Operators tab.
8. Expand the Operators to see we have a variety of operators available:

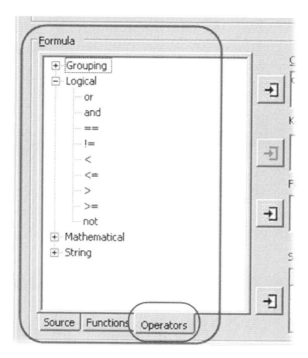

9. Go back to Functions and expand the String functions
10. Select Contains and move it into the Filter Box using the right arrow:

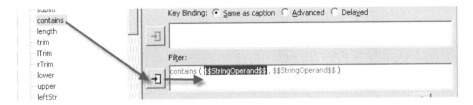

Notice that it shows the parameters using a $$StringOperand$$ notation which indicates the information that you are to complete.

11. Highlight the first $$StringOperand$$ and switch to the source tab:

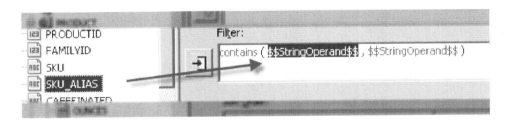

12. Double-click on the member SKU_ALIAS to replace the highlighted parameter.
13. Highlight the second $$StringOperand$$ and replace with "Diet":

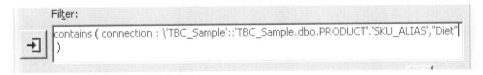

Remember to include the double quotes. This is one of a few oddities of Studio. Text values use double quotes instead of the standard single quotes found in SQL statements.

We also want these members to be sorted in SKU number order.

14. Highlight SKU and click on the right arrow next to Sort Order to move the SKU into the Sort Order box:

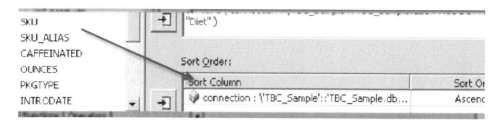

Note that we could change the sort order to descending, but we won't.

15. Click Apply to validate and save the new dimensional element.

If you had no errors, notice that the Key Binding got set to match the Caption Binding (more on bindings in a later section).

16. Verify that your entry looks like the screen below and click OK:

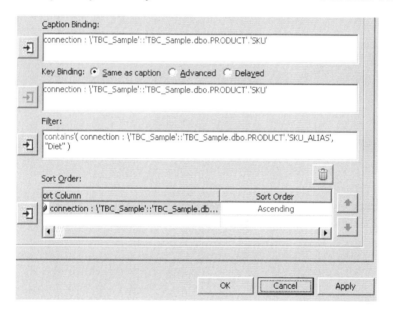

You will notice the dimensional element was added to the Metadata Navigator:

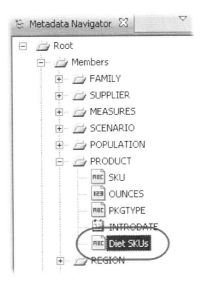

17. Right click on the Diet_SKUs dimensional element and select View Sample Data. If everything worked correctly, you should see the following data set in the working pane of Essbase Studio:

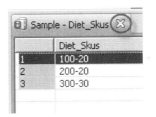

18. Close the sample by clicking on the X of the Sample-Diet_Skus tab.

APPLYING SORT ORDER

Typically we want our members to display in the Essbase outline in a certain order. The sort basis is sometimes alphabetical, other times it is based on member name, along with other possible scenarios. Sorting via Essbase Studio is based on the Dimension Elements. For example, we will have Regions and States in our finished Essbase outline. It would be very nice if the members in the resulting outline were sorted alphabetically to make it easier to find members. So let's do that.

1. Expand Region table to view its columns.
2. Double-click on the Region column and the Properties window will display:

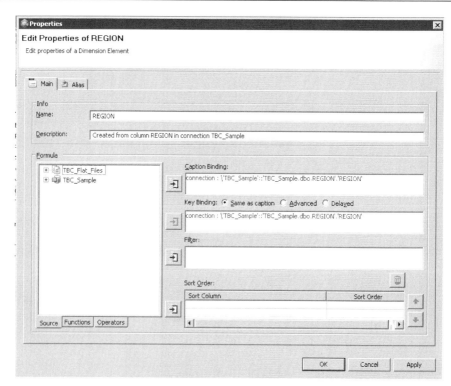

3. In the Formula section on the Source tab, expand to find the Region table and select the column called Region.
4. Using the arrow next to Sort Order, move the column into the Sort Order box:

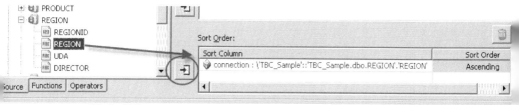

5. Click OK.

If you want to, you can right click on the Region dimensional element in the Metadata Navigator and select Preview Data to see the order of the members. Next go back into the dimensional element properties and change the sort order from Ascending to Descending, save it and preview it again to see how it changed. (Remember to change it back.)

6. Repeat the same steps to apply sorting for the dimensional element STATE in the Market folder.
7. Repeat the same steps to apply sorting for the dimensional element FAMILY in the Family folder.

8. Repeat the same steps to apply sorting for the dimensional element SKU in the Product folder.

Note: When dimensional elements are joined (like Family and SKU, you only need to place the sort on the lowest level.

9. Repeat the same steps to apply sorting for the dimensional element CHILD of the Measures table. This time use SortKey in the sort:

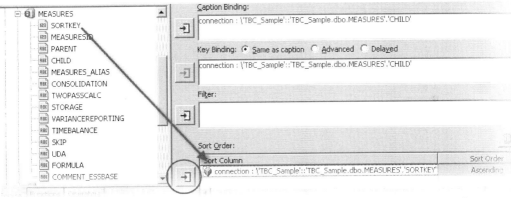

For Parent/Child tables sort keys are a great way to make sure the resulting outline builds the way you expect. This is especially true if you have alternate rollups.

CREATING DATE DIMENSIONAL ELEMENTS

Edward came back from playing with his light saber and said something looked funny. (I suppose he meant something other than him in a Jedi Knight outfit?) He noticed that, for all the members we had, there were none that would make up a Time or Periods dimension. He was, amazingly, correct. I explained to him that there are a number of different ways we can create the members for the Time dimension. First, we can use a dimension table in our relational source that will join to the Transdate column in Sales fact table. Tracy didn't like that idea; since the DBAs had not already built it into the schema, a change request would be required and we all know how long those can take.

I explained that there are two other ways to create a Time dimension without IT help. First, we could create our own dimensional elements based on the Transdate column in the fact table. Second, we could build a date hierarchy. (We will do that eventually in the chapter on Hierarchies, but not until later in the tour.)

Let's test out the first method presented, building the dimensional elements necessary to create a Time dimension.

1. In the Metadata Navigator, right click on the folder called Members and select New>>Folder.

2. Enter the name Periods and click OK.
3. Right click on the newly created Periods folder and select New>>Dimension Element.
4. In the Properties window, enter Month as the name.
5. Select the Functions tab and expand the Date functions.
6. Select monthShortName and move it into the Caption Binding:

7. Replace the $$DateOperand$$ with the connection info for the Transdate column in the Sales table:

8. Click Apply (if you want to validate it) and then click OK.
9. On the newly created Month dimensional element right click and select View Sample Data:

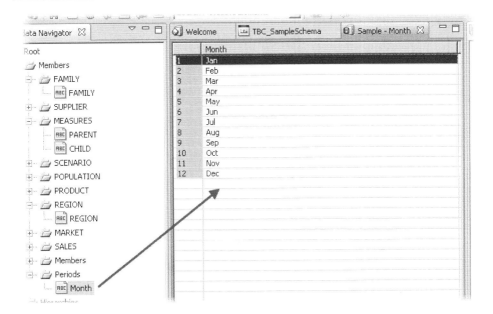

10. Repeat the same steps to create a Quarters dimensional element in the Periods folder using the QuarterAsString function:

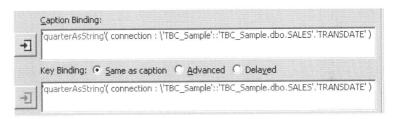

We've now created two dimensional elements that we will be able to use for our Periods dimension.

But wait; there is even an easier way to do this. Just like in school, I've show you the hard way first. Now let's learn a much easier method to create date members.

1. If you created the date elements above, you might want to delete them to do this exercise (or you can change the names in Step 4 below)

2. Drag Transdate from the Sales table in the Data Source Navigator over into the Periods folder you created earlier

3. Righ click on the Transdate member in the periods folder and select "Create Date Elements":

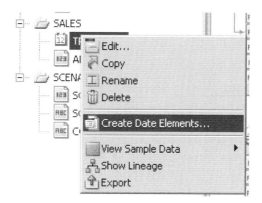

4. Enter Check the selection boxes for Quarter and Month and click OK:

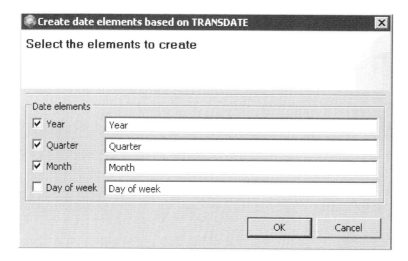

5. The Metadata members are created.

6. If you double click on then you will see they use the same functions as we used to manually create the members.

CREATING TEXT LISTS

As we discussed, in addition to storage of numeric values, Essbase can store text and date type data points in the form of text lists, a list of text values and their associated numeric ids. Remember way back in Chapter 3 when I had you create the table called Sales_Ranking? Probably not, but I did. We created this user defined table to create a text list for our exercises. Follow along.

1. Right click on the Measures Folder under the Members folder and select New>>Text List.
2. In the Properties window that appears enter the name Sales_Ranking.
3. Expand the Bindings in TBC_Sample and expand the table Sales_Ranking.
4. Assign the TABLE_ID column to the ID Binding section.
5. Assign the TABLE_VALUE column to the Value Binding section:

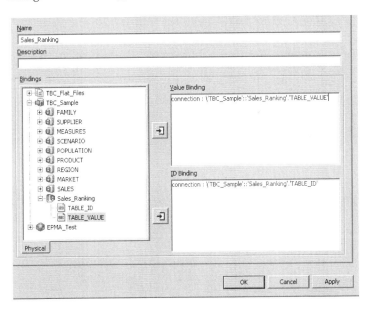

6. Click OK.

You have now successfully created the text list. Easy, wasn't it! It would be nice if you could view sample data for the list, but you currently can't.

CREATING DERIVED TEXT MEASURES

Derived text measures are a special type of text measure that can be used for numeric data elements. These measures are based on predefined ranges. For example, you could define population as shown below as being Small, Medium, Large or Extremely Large:

Low value	High Value	Label
0	6,000,000	Small
6,000,001	18,000,000	Medium
18,000,001	30,000,000	Large
30,000,000	-	Extremely Large

Let's give this a try.

1. Create a folder under Members names User_Defind_Members (we will do this to make them easier to find later)
2. Right click on User_Defined_Members and select New>>Derived Text Measure:

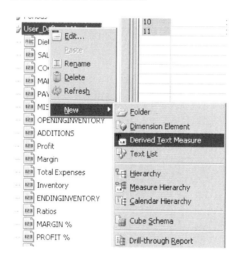

3. Type in the name of the measure. Population_Size into the Name. If you want to, you can enter a description:

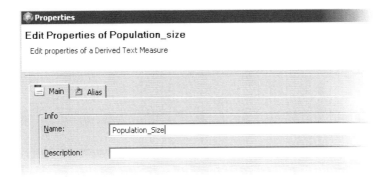

4. Expand the Tree structure TBC_SAMPLE>>Population. Drag the column Population to the Expression box (you can also double click on it):

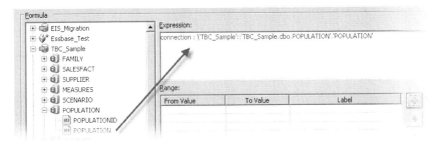

5. Click on the plus sign 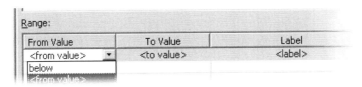 to add values. In the From Value cell drop down the box and select "below" as our first value is anything below 6,000,000. In the To Value enter 6000000 and the label, enter Small:

6. Repeat for the Medium, Large and Extra large ranges as shown in the table above. Remember you have to click the Plus sign each time. If you need to put the members in order, use the up and down arrows. To remove a member use the trash can:

Range: From Value	To Value	Label	
below	6000000	Small	
6000001	18000000	Medium	
18000001	30000000	Large	
30000001	above	Extremely Large	

7. Click OK to save and Exit the form.
8. Find the member Population_Size you just created and right click on it. Select View Sample Data. . The screen will appear. Notice how it added a value for OutofRange. This is a default member in case you have values that fall out of your defined ranges:

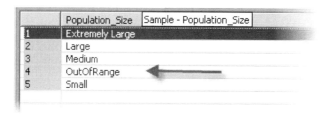

9. Close the Sample data by clicking on the X next to Sample Population_size.

UNDERSTANDING KEY BINDINGS

Key bindings are the way Studio selects the member to be loaded from the source. When you create a Dimension Element, you can associate three different types of bindings: "Same as Caption", "Advanced" and "Delayed".

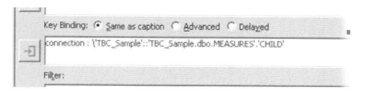

Same as Caption

This is the default binding type. When selected, Studio copies whatever was put into the caption binding expression into the Key binding. It is typically used when you know that duplicate member names will not be used in created outlines.

Advanced

This option is used in two cases. First, when you have duplicate member names enabled for a database. Second, it is automatically set when the data type of a member in the caption binding is anything other than text. In these instances, you would provide an expression that produces a unique identifier to be passed to Essbase. As an example, in a geography dimension, you have a column for City. You have the city name "Riverside" that is duplicated 46 times (because this is a city in all but 4 states). In your table, you also have a column called CityID that uniquely identifies the cities. Ideally in the source, this would be a key or foreign key. In most cases when using advanced, the value in the binding will be a numeric type and will differ from the caption binding.

Delayed

Delayed bindings can be used on either duplicate or unique member hierarchies. This type of binding is used when you are unsure of how to create the key binding. It allows Studio to automatically create the binding. The key binding can also be manually created during hierarchy creation or maintenance. When Studio creates the binding, or you do it manually, the full path for the members participating in the binding are used. For example: for the Product hierarchy, there are two members Family and SKU. Using the same as caption setting, the two members have bindings of:

```
Family - connection :
\'TBC_Sample'::'TBC_Sample.dbo.FAMILY'.'FAMILY'
SKU - connection :
\'TBC_Sample'::'TBC_Sample.dbo.PRODUCT'.'SKU'
```

If we change the binding for the SKU member, based on my folder structure, the binding Studio creates would look something like:

```
class :
\'TBC_Sample'\'Members'\'FAMILY'\'FAMILY'.'caption'
|| "_" || class :
\'TBC_Sample'\'Members'\'PRODUCT'\'SKU'.'caption'
```

When you change it, Studio will warn you about the change. If you accept changes, Studio will update the hierarchies using that member. In addition, within the hierarchy, the member is now editable:

When using delayed key bindings, the binding expression for the member is left blank.

Outfitted in his new costume, his pockets full of souvenir key bindings (he liked how shiny they were) and his new found knowledge of how to work with Dimension members; Edward was ready to move on. But where are we to go next? It is only logical that we combine those Dimension members together to create hierarchies. Where better to go than to Set Design and Building.

Chapter 6:
Set Design & Build

The tour was going more quickly than Edward and Tracy expected. They thought Studio would be hard to figure out, but it had so far proven to be much easier than they expected. Tracy was excited about this and Edward even more so; he had hopes of making it to the theme park before they sold out of sorbet. We were back on the tram headed to the Set Building department. "On your left is the famous Arbor tree," was droning over the loud speaker. Edward looked confused and Tracy chuckled at the reference. Tracy was trying to second-guess what Set Design was all about. She thought it would be where we took the Dimension Elements and assigned attributes to them, like formulas and consolidation tags. It was a good guess, but not correct.

The Set Design department is where we take the different Dimension Elements we created and put them together into Hierarchies to be used in Essbase cubes. The nice thing about Hierarchies is that they are generic, so you can build them once and use them in multiple cubes. It saves time recreating them for every cube that you are maintaining. "Building hierarchies in Studio is different from building them in EAS," I explained. In EAS you type the actual member names into the outline (e.g. "Cola", "Diet Cola", or "Root Beer"). In Studio you use the columns or dimensional elements to define the hierarchies (e.g. FAMILY, SKU). Essbase Studio can build three types of hierarchies:

- Standard Hierarchies
- Calendar Hierarchies
- Measures Hierarchies

I promised they would see all three hierarchy types on the tour along with some fun attractions like alternate hierarchies and attribute dimension creation.

CREATING A STANDARD HIERARCHY

Standard hierarchies are the foundation of your cube structures. Most hierarchies created within Essbase Studio will be standard hierarchies. This type of hierarchy combines physical, logical and user defined elements to create the structure of your cubes. Standard hierarchies can contain both alternate rollups and attribute dimension rollups.

To create a standard hierarchy,

1. From the Metadata Navigator, right click on the folder we created called Hierarchies and select New>>Hierarchy.

The Hierarchy editor will display. Before we move forward, let's review the features and functions of the Hierarchy Editor. First, you can move columns to be children of other columns or back as siblings. You can also delete them using icons in the tool bar:

So if you don't first place your columns correctly, you can move them as needed. A word of warning: if you delete a parent, all of the children below it will be deleted as well.

You can next move the position of columns either up or down by using the up and down arrows. Columns must be at the same indentation level to move them up or down:

Next, you can save, cancel, or preview your hierarchy, or add elements to it using the buttons below. Don't worry; when you save a hierarchy, the cancel button turns into a close button so you can exit the editor without canceling:

Finally, with the Add button, you can add columns or user defined columns (hard coding) to the hierarchy:

Now that we have had a mini-tour of the screen, let's get back to work.

2. In the Hierarchy Editor, name the Hierarchy Market. The name entered is the default hierarchy name used in cube building; it can be changed later if desired.

3. Expand the Members folder in the Metadata Navigator and expand Region and Market.

4. From the Region folder drag the Region column into the Hierarchy editor:

5. Next, from the Market folder, drag the State column, placing your cursor on the already placed Region member. If done correctly, the State will be placed as a child of Region (indented). If not, just use the right arrow to indent it:

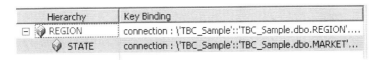

6. Click on the Preview button. You should see the following hierarchy:

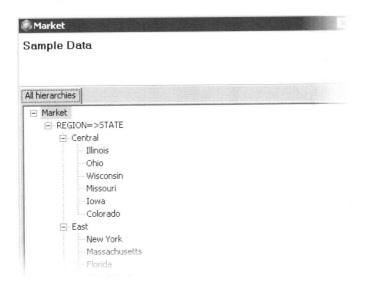

7. Close the preview and click Save.

CREATING AN ALTERNATE HIERARCHY

Next, we want to create the Products hierarchy. In the case of products, we have an alternate rollup of Diet Drinks and a number of associated attribute dimensions. To create the alternate hierarchy we will need to add a user defined member called Diet Drinks.

1. Just like we did for Market, right click on the Hierarchies folder and select New>>Hierarchy.
2. Name the hierarchy Products.
3. Drag the member Family into the Hierarchy editor and drag SKU into the editor as a child of Family:

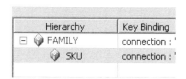

4. Preview the data and it will look like this:

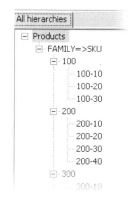

5. Close the preview.
6. With the member Family in the editor highlighted, click the Add button. Select Add user- defined sibling:

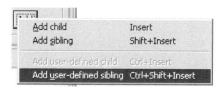

7. Type "Diet Drinks" for "New Member".

Don't worry that the binding says "Unspecified" for the Diet Drinks. The binding will be addressed once we save the hierarchy.

8. Drag the column Diet_SKUs that we created earlier from the Product folder to be a child of Diet Drinks:

Hierarchy	Key Binding
⊟ 🔷 FAMILY	connection : \'TBC_Sample'::'TBC
🔷 SKU	connection : \'TBC_Sample'::'TBC
⊟ 🔷 Diet Drinks	Unspecified
🔷 Diet_Skus	connection : \'TBC_Sample'::'TBC

9. Preview the hierarchy and you should see both the primary rollup and the alternate rollup:

```
⊟ 400
     400-10
     400-20
     400-30
⊟ Diet Drinks=>Diet_Skus
  ⊟ Diet Drinks
       100-20
```

10. Close the preview and click Save on the editor.

CREATING AN ATTRIBUTE DIMENSION

Alternate rollups and attribute dimensions are built very similarly within a hierarchy; it is not until we get to the Essbase properties that we differentiate Attribute Dimensions. When you create an attribute dimension in a hierarchy, the base member that the attribute dimension associates with **MUST** be the child of the attribute. So let's build some attributes.

1. If the Hierarchy Editor for the Product hierarchy is not open, double click in the Metadata Navigator on the Product hierarchy created in the previous steps.
2. Drag Ounces over to be a sibling of Family.
3. Drag SKU (the base members) to be a child of Ounces. Preview the data. Doesn't this look just like the Diet Drinks alternate rollup?

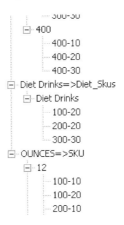

```
     300-30
⊟ 400
     400-10
     400-20
     400-30
⊟ Diet Drinks=>Diet_Skus
  ⊟ Diet Drinks
       100-20
       200-20
       300-30
⊟ OUNCES=>SKU
  ⊟ 12
       100-10
       100-20
       200-10
```

4. Repeat the steps for Pkgtype, IntroDate, and Caffeinated columns, adding them as a sibling to Family and SKU as a child. Preview the hierarchy. It should look as follows:

Tip!

If you forget to put the base member as a child of the Attribute dimension, you will not be able to designate it as an attribute dimension later.

5. Save and close the Hierarchy Editor.
6. Right click on the Hierarchies folder and select New>>Hierarchy:

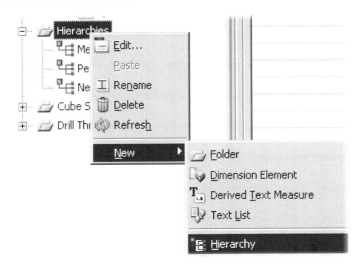

7. Repeat the steps above to create the Measures hierarchy using the Standard Hierarchy editor. (We will do it using a Measures Hierarchy build later.) The members you need are Parent and Child.

8. Preview the Measures hierarchy to make sure it looks correct then save it (Click Save and then Close):

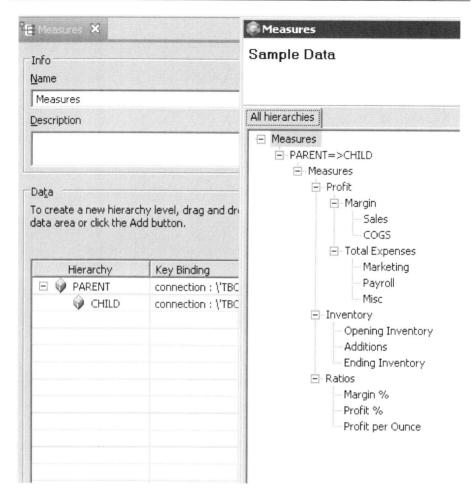

9. Right click on the Hierarchies folder and select New>>Hierarchy:
10. Repeat the steps above to create the Periods hierarchy using the Standard Hierarchy editor. (We will do it using a Measures Hierarchy build later.) The columns you need are Quarters and Months.
11. Preview the Periods hierarchy to make sure it looks correct then save it:

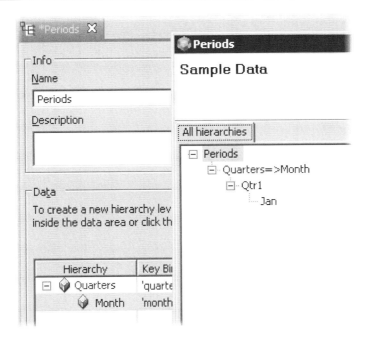

When you are done, you should have a Hierarchies folder that looks like the following:

Notice the member Diet Drinks in the folder. This is the user-defined member we created when we created our alternate rollup for Products. For every user-defined member you create, Studio will build a member. This member can be used in any hierarchy. If you like, you can drag this into the Members folder. (I actually like to create a folder for them called User_Defined_Members).

12. Right click on the Hierarchies folder and select New>>Hierarchy:

13. Repeat the steps above to create the Scenario hierarchy using the Standard Hierarchy editor. Use the Dimension member called Scenario and drag it over:

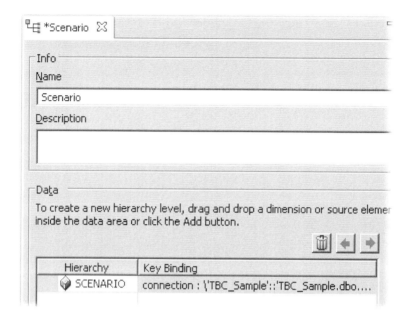

14. Click the Add button and select Add user-defined sibling:

15. Type in "Variance":

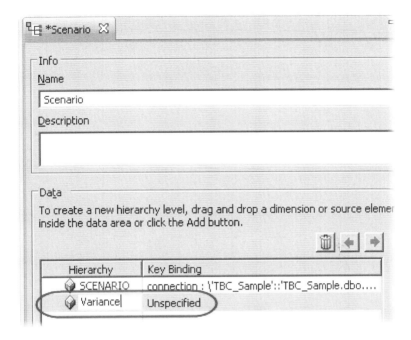

16. Click the Add button and select Add user-defined sibling:

17. Type in "Variance %". The resulting Scenario hierarchy should look as follows:

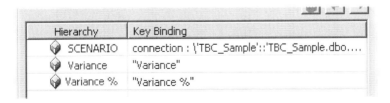

18. Like before, save the changes and close the editor.

Now that you are an expert at regular hierarchies, let's turn our attention to Calendar hierarchies.

CALENDAR HIERARCHIES

When we were looking at Dimension Elements, I showed Edward and Tracy how they could create columns based on a date field in the relational source. I told them there was another way to build Time dimensions using calendar hierarchies (more of a wizard driven process). The creation of the calendar hierarchy is independent of the data within your source, but gets tied to it later based on the lowest level within the hierarchy you choose.

The process allows you to define a calendar based on different calendar types. These types include:

- Gregorian
- Fiscal
- Retail
- ISO
- Manufacturing

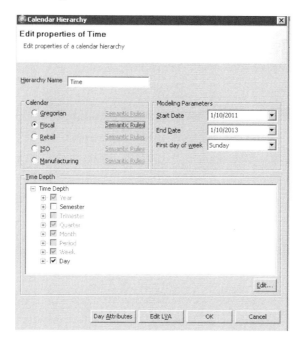

For each calendar type, a predefined set of hierarchy members is defined. You can modify the hierarchy (in some cases) to add or remove levels to fit your needs. . For example: if you select Gregorian, you are presented with Year and Month as required levels. You can, if you wish, also choose Semester, Trimester, Week and Day as levels. If you select ISO, the wizard defaults to Year, Month and Day, and I can't change any of them nor can you add additional levels.

You also set the range of dates for the dimension. In other words, you select the beginning and ending calendar dates to be considered when building the dimension. For some of the types (Fiscal, Retail and Manufacturing) you also have the ability to set semantic rules to further define how the calendar gets built. For example, in a Fiscal calendar you get the selections shown below (I think a picture here is probably better than me trying to describe it):

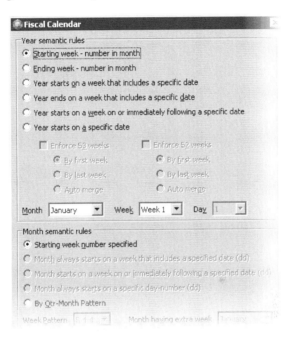

There are two other important features of creating a calendar hierarchy. The process allows you to create Day Attributes and Linked Value Attributes. I explained to Edward how important this might be for analyzing his data. It is most likely that his business has peaks on weekends and holidays. By defining these as attributes, he can analyze the data more easily. While he could do this analysis in other ways, the Calendar hierarchy makes it easy to create the comparison points. Similarly, Linked Value Attributes create associations based on a shared pattern of time, such as the first month of every quarter or the last week of every month.

Let's actually create a Time dimension for Edward with the following requirements. It will be based on a Gregorian calendar. His Year starts in Jan 1st since he loves the to dress in a diaper and pretend he is the new year baby. His business uses a monthly calendar. The calendar should be for 3 years starting in 2010. He wants to be able to report on Saturdays and Sundays and holidays, so we need the system to break them out. The holidays that are big money makers for him are New Year's

Day and July 4th. The calendar needs to go to the day level. Edward cares about weeks and quarters. He has not decided if he wants to do year over year reporting for the same week. So let's get started.

1. Right click on the folder Hierarchies and select New>>Calendar Hierarchy.
2. In the dialog that comes up enter the Hierarchy name Time (aren't I imaginative?).
3. Select each of the calendar types and look at the default selected time depths.
4. Click on the semantic rules (if available) to see what selections are available.
5. Select Retail.
6. Set the Start date to be 1/1/2010 and the End date to be 12/31/2012.
7. Set Monday as the first day of the week. Notice that on the Time depth you can add semester but nothing else:

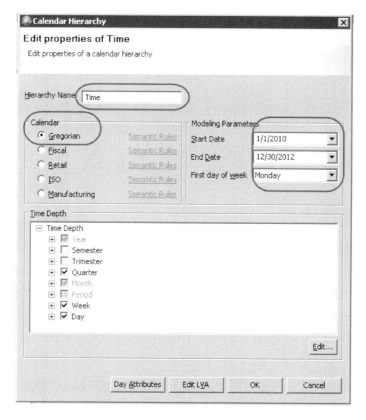

8. Click on Day Attributes button.
9. Check Saturday and Sunday and give them the dimension name Weekend.

10. Under Holidays add the following then click OK.
    a. Jan 1, 2011
    b. Jan 1, 2012
    c. Jan 1, 2013
    d. July 4, 2010
    e. July 4, 2011
    f. July 4, 2012

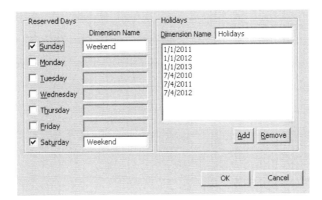

11. Click OK.
12. Click on Edit LVA.
13. Check the Week in Year and change the Dimension name to Week_In_Year and the Alias Prefix to WIY_. (We are giving Edward some functionality just in case):

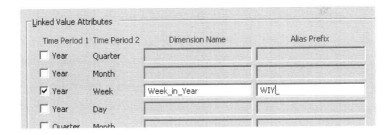

14. Click OK.
15. Click OK to close the Calendar Hierarchy. Notice we have a hierarchy named Time with a little clock to signify that it is a time dimension:

16. Right click on the Time hierarchy and select Preview data. You will see the following:

Looks pretty ugly; let's pretty it up a bit.

17. Close the Preview.
18. Edit the Time hierarchy. (Double-click on it or right click and select Edit).
19. Expand out the Year in the Time Depth and highlight the Labeling Rule then click Edit:

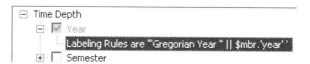

20. Select RY Year 2006 and click OK.
21. Repeat for Quarter, Month and Day, selecting how you want the members to look. In my case I selected:
    - Quarter 1 2006
    - January 2006
    - 01/02/06
22. Edward decided he doesn't need weeks, so uncheck weeks.
23. When done, click OK to save your changes and preview the data to see what it will look like.

Tip!

You cannot create a custom format here. You are limited to the formats supplied.

Here is what my preview looked like after changes. I think it looks a lot better:

Notice something odd? It looks like it did before I made any changes. The preview appears to be a bit buggy. Once in a while it will show you the formatting you selected, but most of the time it won't. Hopefully this is resolved in the next version.

MEASURES HIERARCHIES

Measures Hierarchies are used when your fact table has multiple columns that hold the data. For example, if your fact table contained columns for sales, Expenses, Inventory, etc. you would want to consider building an Accounts Hierarchy. If you want to attempt the following exercise, you will need to add the table SalesFact to the data source. (Hint: right click on the data source TBC_Sample and look at Incremental Update). In this table the columns to create the base members for the Accounts dimension of Sample Basic are included. Once the table is added, we can create the hierarchy from it. We want to replicate what was created in the Measures hierarchy we created earlier; if you want to look at it, you can preview the data from it. If you are lazy, I've shown it below:

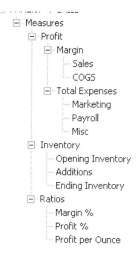

Tip!

I prefer to build the hierarchy as a standard hierarchy - I think it gives me more flexibility - but if you have a simple accounts dimension building an Accounts hierarchy may be easier.

1. With your cursor on the Hierarchies folder, right click and select New>>Measure Hierarchy.
2. In the Measures Hierarchy dialogue that appears, enter AccountFact as the name.
3. Expand out the TBC_Sample Data Source (Right Pane) and expand the table SalesFact. (Notice that we do not have columns for Profit, Margin, Total Expenses, Inventory, or Ratios; we will have to manually create those.)
4. Click on the Add button and add a user-defined Child.
5. Rename it Profit.
6. Repeat for Margin.
7. Select Margin and click the Add>>Add a user-defined sibling, naming the member "Total Expenses".
8. Select Profit and click the Add>>Add a user-defined sibling, naming the member "Inventory".
9. Select Profit and click the Add>>Add a user-defined sibling, naming the member "Ratios".

The resulting hierarchy should look as follows:

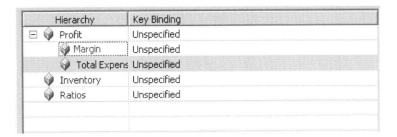

Tip!

If you get the order or indentation wrong, use the arrows to move the members to the correct location in the hierarchy.

10. From the SalesFact Table, drag the Sales column into the editor, placing it on the Margin member. (If done correctly, it will be added as a child of Margin).
11. Repeat for Cogs, Marketing, Payroll, etc., placing the members under the correct parent members:

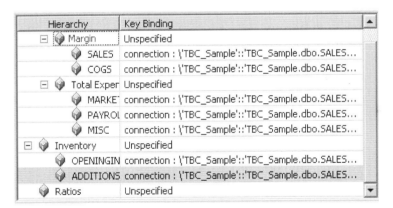

12. Create the manual members for Ending Inventory, Margin %, Profit % and Profit per ounce and put them into the correct places.
13. Click Save to save the Hierarchy.
14. Click Close.
Notice that in the Hierarchies folder we now have a lot of new members. Since these members did not exist in the Metadata Navigator, Studio added them in the folder we were working in. If you like, you can move them to the Members folder.
15. Right click on the AccountFact Hierarchy and select Preview Hierarchy.
What's that? It's greyed out? That is because you can't preview Measure Hierarchies. Fooled you, didn't I?

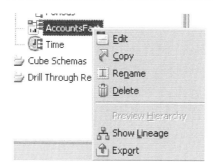

   I had to get Edward's attention as he had started playing with his light saber again and Tracy was getting antsy. She thought all of this was interesting, but she's a result oriented gal. She wanted to get to the point of actually being able to get her hands on what she dearly wanted. (No, that was not wrapped tightly around Edward's neck, although I'll bet some days it was.) She wanted to see how the Essbase cube would really be built. I told her we were almost there and I corralled them back onto the tram to head off to our next site.

Chapter 7:
Dubbing

We took a small detour and headed over to the music studio where dubbing would occur. As we walked in we met a long-haired geezer crooning out Frank Sinatra tunes. I introduced Edward and Tracy to Rich, our head dubber. I warned them that they would have to talk loudly since Rich spent way too many nights in front of amps and his hearing was shot. I asked Rich to explain what happened in dubbing. Instead of telling them that this is where we create Alias Sets and associate aliases to the members, he broke out into a song:

And now, the end is near;
And so I create the final members.
My friend, I'll say it clear,
I'll state my case, of which I'm certain.

I've built an alias set that's full.
I've named each and ev'ry member;
But more, much more than this,
I did it my way.

Aliases, I've had a few;
But then again, each adds clarity.
I did what I had to do
And saw it through for user clarity.

I planned each Alias set;
Each alias set along the hierarchy,
But more, much more than this,
I did it my way.

Yes, there were times, I'm sure you knew
When I bit off more than I could chew.
But through it all, when there was doubt,
I ate it up and spit it out.
I faced it all and I stood tall;
And did it my way.

I tried to interrupt him, but he just ignored us and kept singing. He didn't even realize I'd ushered Edward and Tracy into the dubbing studio and locked the door so he could not get in. I interpreted Rich's song into something Tracy and Edward could understand. Our dubbing department takes the individual Dimensional Elements and associates multiple aliases to them. If you think of dubbing a film, you add languages the viewer will understand. Just like that, Aliases add descriptions that users will better understand. Each alias for a member is part of an Alias set like words are part of a language. In Essbase 11.1.2 you can have up to 32 alias sets associated to a member within an Essbase database (10 in older versions). What is nice is that you can decide by Essbase model what alias sets you want to use for a dimensional element. So you define the Alias Sets once and use them over and over again, just like dimensional elements and hierarchies.

Alias sets are containers to group the aliases for individual dimensional elements. Follow the directions below to create an Alias set.

If you are using version 11.1.2.2 skip down to the section Creating an Alias Set in Version 11.1.2.2

CREATING AN ALIAS SET PRIOR TO VERSION 11.1.2.2

1. From the Studio menu select Tools>>Alias Set Manager:

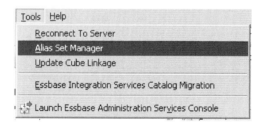

2. Right click on the Plus button:

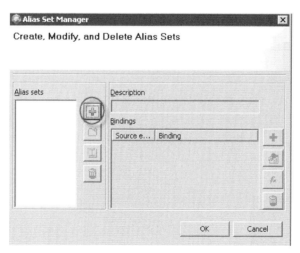

3. Enter a name for the Alias set (I used Default) then click the OK button:

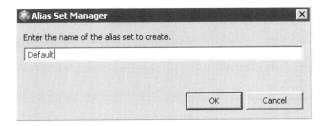

Tip!

Although you can't find it in the documentation, to create the default alias table, name the alias set "default" and apply it in your Essbase model. Who would have thought it was that easy!

The Alias set container has now been created. Once created, notice that the options to copy, rename or delete the Alias set are available:

It is that easy to create the Alias set. Granted, we have not created any aliases yet; that is still to come. Skip over the next section to Creating Aliases. Why? Because by reading this "Prior to 11.1.2.2" section, you've told me you are not on version 11.1.2.2 (yet) so there is no reason to read the next section.

CREATING AN ALIAS SET IN TO VERSION 11.1.2.2

In version 11.1.2.2 alias sets are created within the Metadata Navigator not the tools menu. It is interesting (to me) that alias sets can be created within individual folders and as global objects. This means you can have multiple alias sets with the same name with different aliases in them. Notice how Default exists in both the root and TBC_Sample folders below.

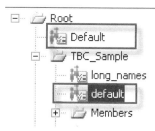

Even though you can have multiple alias sets with the same name, you can't use two Alias sets with the same name in one Essbase model. If you have a global Alias set called Default and an Alias set called Default in another folder, you will get errors when trying to save the Essbase Model if you use both in the Model. According to the documentation, in the Essbase model properties you can rename one of the alias sets. Unfortunately, when I attempted to do a rename, Studio would not allow me to do so.

Tip!

While you can create alias sets with duplicate names, a best practice is to keep the names unique. In the Essbase cube properties, you decide what alias sets to use and there is a new option for "Name in cube". In addition, due to issues, we still recommend putting your alias sets in the root if the Metadata Navigator.

To create an alias set:
1. From the Metadata Navigator, navigate to the folder where you want to create the Alias Set.
2. Right click on the folder and select New->Alias Set.
3. The following dialog appears:

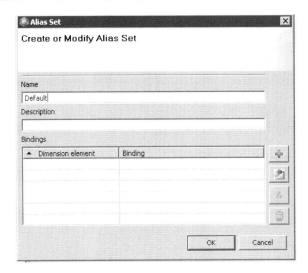

4. Enter a name for the Alias Set. If you want it to be used as the default aliases in your Essbase cube name it "Default" (See tip above). Give it a description if you like.

CREATING ALIASES

Once an Alias set has been created, you can populate it with the relationships between dimensional elements and their respective descriptions. There are two ways to create the aliases: first, from introspection, and second, manually. While you can always build all aliases manually, if you use introspection, you may also need to use manual creation. While the screen is slightly different in version 11.1.2.2, the steps are basically the same. You can use inspection or manually create them.

Aliases by Inspection

Many of the associations between dimensional elements and aliases can be created automatically just like the joins between tables. Let's see how that is done.

1. If you closed down the Alias set manager, reopen it and highlight the default alias set.
2. Click on the Inspect button:

3. In the Pattern for Alias column, enter *ALIAS and select the TBC_Sample data source:

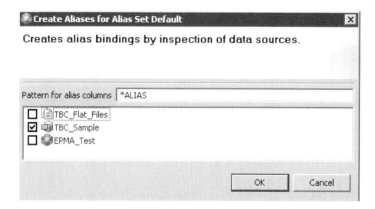

4. Click OK.

Tip!

Prior to 11.1.2.2 the pattern is case sensitive so Alias will not return the same results as ALIAS. The pattern also allows for wildcards in the names. Again, ALIAS would not be the same as *ALIAS.

Notice that a number of source elements and bindings are now populated:

Bindings

Source element	Binding
Diet_Skus	connection : \'TBC_Sample'::'TBC_...
FAMILY	connection : \'TBC_Sample'::'TBC_...
POPULATION	connection : \'TBC_Sample'::'TBC_...
SKU	connection : \'TBC_Sample'::'TBC_...

If you want to look at one of them, highlight it and press the function button. When you're finished looking, close the Function Editor.

5. Select the SKU column and click the FX button:

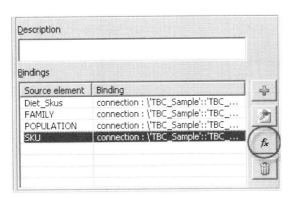

If you look at the above screen you will see we created aliases for a number of dimensional elements: Diet_Skus, FAMILY, POPULATION, and SKU. You may have different ones based on how you built your Metadata members, but there is definitely something missing. We do not have anything for our Measures. We will need to add this manually. To add a manual association click on the Add button (+ sign).

6. Click on the Add button (+ sign).

7. In the source selection tree, navigate to TBC_Sample>>Members>>Measures and expand it.

8. Highlight Child dimensional element and the binding expression tree will populate.

9. Expand the Measures table and click on Measures_Alias.

See how it populated into the Binding expression located at the top of the screen?

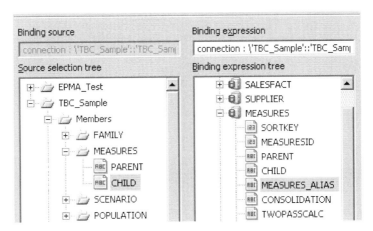

10. Click OK to save the binding.

Tip!

If you click on OK and the screen just sits there, it most likely means you are trying to add an association to a dimensional element that already exists. Studio gives you no message about this. Cancel the association and check the list of bindings.

11. Click OK to save and close the Alias Set manager.

Using the Function Editor you can modify the alias names, doing things like concatenating two columns together to create the alias, sub stringing a selected column, or a number of other things. While this is doable, if you are planning on using Drill Through, it is better to do these types of modifications in your source and pass them to Studio.

If you are on version 11.1.2.2, make sure to read this next section about the specifics of creating aliases in 11.1.2.2.

Creating Aliases in 11.1.2.2

If you are using 11.1.2.2, you can use the steps illustrated above. However you need to know about an additional feature available in 11.1.2.2. Alias sets can span data sources and minischemas. A few challenges occur with this design, you might not know what the actual metadata element is pointing to. If you have a member called "Child" from from the measures table in a source called TBC Sample and an a member called Child from a source TBC1, Essbase Studio displays both as "Child". Second, the members are intermingled.

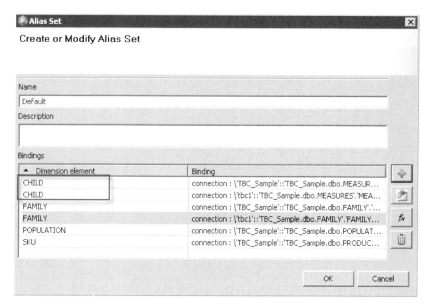

Now you're saying "Thanks, Glenn. Now what do I do about it?"

Would I bring this up if there wasn't a solution? You know me too well; of course I would, but not this time.

In 11.1.2.2 right click on the Alias set and the following window will display:

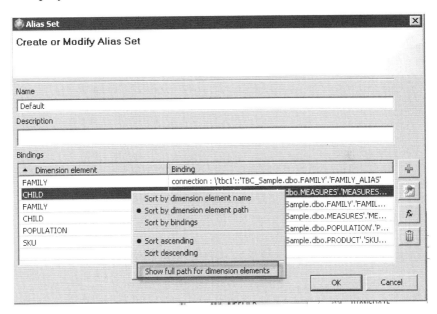

Notice you can sort by dimension element name,imension element path, or bindings in assending or descending order. These features make it easier to group your alias elements. Also (and more important to me) is the last option to show the full path of the dimension elements. When you select this option, notice the screen changes to show the full path:

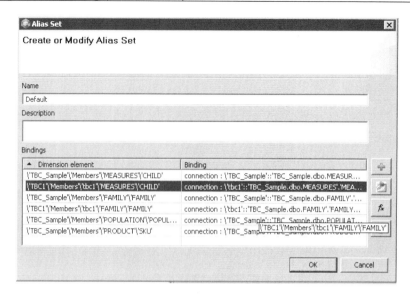

You can now easily tell which source "Child" now refers to in the measures element.

When we get to Chapter 8, we will discuss how we can work with Alias sets in the Essbase model properties along with additional functionality for DTS members.

ADDING ALIASES TO USER DEFINED MEMBERS

Remember when we created some manual dimensional elements, such as the member "Diet Drinks"? If you edited the properties for the user defined member, you would have noticed a tab for Alias but you were not able to edit it. This is because we did not have any Alias sets defined to allow for updating the alias. Now that we have at least one Alias set defined, we can go back and add an alias to this user defined member.

1. Locate the dimension element Diet Drinks in the Metadata Navigator. Double click on it.

2. Click on the Alias tab. Notice how the Default Alias set is listed:

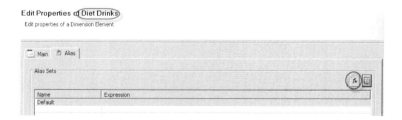

3. Click on the function button.

4. In the screen that appears, enter "Diet Soft Drinks". Remember to include the quotes or you will get an error:

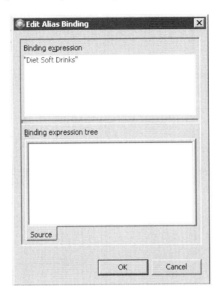

5. Click OK.

The binding will be added. For user-defined members, there is no binding expression tree, nor can you use functions to create members. These are hard coded:

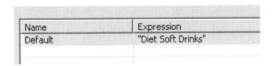

Tip!

Once the Alias set is created, you can add the aliases to dimensional elements when you edit them just like you can for user defined members.

As we were leaving the dubbing studio we could hear Rich droning in the background:

This is my kind of cube, BSO is;
My kind of cube, BSO is.
My kind of Aliases too,
Where members associate to.

Each time I roam, BSO is
Calling me home, BSO is
Why can't I just grin like a clown

It's my kind of sound

With that we ran, not walked, to the tram and headed off to Makeup.

Chapter 8:
Makeup

After our interesting experience in dubbing, Edward and Tracy were looking for a little more sanity in the Studio. Since we were going to Makeup, I wasn't sure I could provide that. Makeup is where we put the needed hierarchies together and define the Essbase properties; in a sense we "makeup" our cubes here. I thought it was funny as I chuckled to myself. Edward and Tracy just stared at me blankly. OK, I figured I had better bring in someone who could relate to them better, so I hurried them forward so I would not have to say much more. We turned the corner and there she was: Danielle, our chief makeup artist. She was busy flipping quarters with her boss for a raise. Poor sap, he did not know what he was in for. Like most things, she was a pro at this bar game. How much time did she spend in bars? Hmmm, I never thought of that before.

You could see Edwards eyes light up at this diminutive blond bombshell. I could tell what Edward was thinking, so before things went from bad to worse, I reminded him that I had said "Makeup artist" not "Make out artist". Tracy looked awestruck. She immediately introduced herself to Danielle like Danielle was a superstar. I don't know why, but everyone who has heard about the Studio seems to know Danielle. I don't understand, but perhaps I should move her to publicity or training. She seems to be the face of the Studio.

Danielle professionally ignored my comments (oh good, no HR visit for me today) and explained what she does in Makeup. She selects hierarchies that were created in Set Design and brings them together to make up a Cube Schema. The Cube Schema is the foundational building block for creating an Essbase cube. It is made up of metadata elements such as measures and hierarchies.

From the cube schema, you generate (or "makeup") one or more Essbase Models. An Essbase model creates a graphical representation of the cube schema. After an Essbase Model is created, the Makeup department defines the Essbase model properties; things like consolidation operators, alias tables, formulas, UDAs and other properties are edited, making the cubes ready for show time.

One cube schema can be used to create multiple Essbase models, and each Essbase model can create the same cube on multiple servers. This reduces the need for maintenance.

Danielle also explained that Makeup only goes so far when it comes to defining Essbase cube properties. To set some cube properties like index and data caches, volumes used, and partitions , you have to go to our sister company EAS (Essbase Administration Services). Danielle explained EAS and Essbase Studio work closely to make the application shine.

Needless to say, I understand why Tracy was impressed; this lady knows her stuff. She explained step by step how to build the schema and edit the Essbase properties. I am always amazed at how much I learn from her.

BUILDING THE CUBE SCHEMA

The cube schema is an amalgamation of measures and hierarchies. When we build a schema, we first define what are our measures are. Measures can be individual dimension elements, a group of elements or an accounts hierarchy. Danielle told us that individual dimension elements are called "loose" measures in the documentation. To prevent me getting more HR meetings than I deserve, make up your own jokes about the term". You can only add only one Measures hierarchy but you can add multiple loose measures.

We then choose which hierarchies we are going to include in the schema. Optionally, we can preview these hierarchies after they are added.

To build the cube schema,

1. Right click on the folder Cube Schemas and select New>>Cube Schema.
2. Enter the name of the schema as TBC_Sample.
3. Expand out the TBC_Samples folder, then the Sales Folder.

The first major step in creating the cube schema, as mentioned above, is adding measures. We will be using a loose measure to build our model. You need to have at least one measure in your model. It is required so Studio knows where to get the "data" values from when creating data load SQL statements.

4. Select the member Amount (It is in the Sales Dimension members folder if you followed my examples. If not, you will have to add the sales table to your minischema and, create the joins and then create the Dimension member). Move the amount member into the Measures/Measures Hierarchies box using the right arrow (or drag it over):

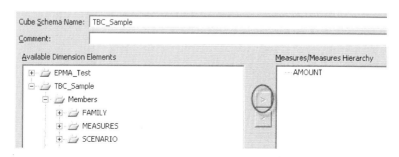

5. Close the Members folder and expand the Hierarchies folder.
6. Select and move the following hierarchies into the Hierarchies box (Measures, Periods, Scenario, Products, Markets:

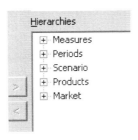

If you wish, you can click on Preview hierarchies to see what the hierarchies look like (you did this when you created the hierarchies). If you do this, review the hierarchies and then close the preview window.

7. Click Next.

If you created a calendar hierarchy or need to associate the data with manually created members, check the Override default data load bindings:

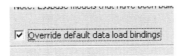

We did not have this, so you can leave it unchecked.

8. Check the Create Essbase Model Box. You can leave the name the same.
9. In the Accounts dimension dropdown, change from system default to Measures:

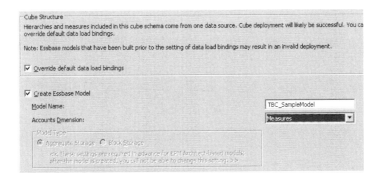

If you had used a measures hierarchy as the measures in the cube schema build, the accounts dimension will be set to "System default". You will not be allowed to change this option. If you have used loose members, then you are allowed to select what hierarchy you want your accounts dimension to be built from in the Essbase model.

10. Click Finish.

Congratulations, you have your first cube schema! Isn't she adorable?

Override Default Data

If you choose the Override default data load bindings option in the Cube Schema wizard, you will click Next instead of Finish to define override connection information. To give you an example, I created a new cube schema using the Time hierarchy (we created this as a Calendar hierarchy). When you click Next after saying Override default data, you will see:

Notice the data load binding for Day is blank or empty. If you try to build an Essbase model without specifying the binding, it will fail. To create the binding, double click on the desired Data Load Bindings row and the ... button will appear. Select this button to edit the bindings. The following screen will display:

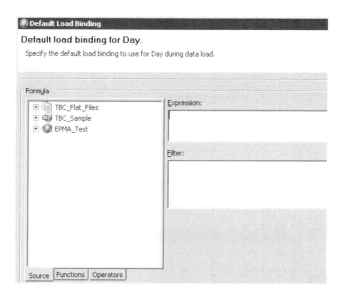

Note that this screen is similar to the creation of dimensional elements interface. We will need to use columns and functions to create a member that is the same format as our dimensional element for day (mm/dd/yyyy). Below is the formula I used to achieve this. Remember, we are limited to the functions and operators available in Studio, not all the SQL expressions. I used date operators in conjunction with concatenation operators and hard coded vales to get the format I wanted:

```
'month' ( connection :
\'TBC_Sample'::'TBC_Sample.dbo.SALES'.'TRANSDATE' )
|| "/" || 'weekday' (connection :
\'TBC_Sample'::'TBC_Sample.dbo.SALES'.'TRANSDATE' )
|| "/" || 'year' ( connection :
\'TBC_Sample'::'TBC_Sample.dbo.SALES'.'TRANSDATE' )
```

Expression:
```
'month' (connection : \'TBC_Sample'::'TBC_Sample.dbo.SALES'.'TRANSDATE' )
|| "/" || 'weekday' ( connection : \'TBC_Sample'::'TBC_Sample.dbo.SALES'.'TRANSDATE' ) || "/"
|| 'year' ( connection : \'TBC_Sample'::'TBC_Sample.dbo.SALES'.'TRANSDATE'|)
```

When you click OK, the formula gets added to the binding. Then, if you click Finish, the Essbase model is created.

THE ESSBASE MODEL

When you click Finish on the Cube Schema wizard, the Essbase model will be created (since we told the wizard to build it). Two visible changes will occur. First, a graphical representation of the models with its hierarchies will be shown in the working pane. Second, the cube schema with the model as a child of the schema will be shown in the Metadata Navigator:

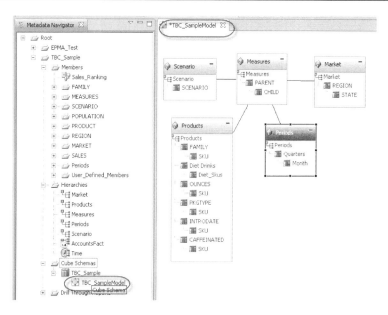

Edward was confused. He had seen Essbase a lot (his twin brother by the same name even wrote a book about it). This did not look anything like the Essbase databases he had seen before. Where's the outline? Where are the hierarchy members? He was right; this does not look the same, yet. When we build Essbase models in Essbase Studio, we are building and structuring the underlying metadata to generate a normal Essbase cube with the actual members. Once we deploy an Essbase model, we will see the fruits of our labors in the resulting Essbase outline (more on those steps on our Distribution stop).

EDITING ESSBASE PROPERTIES

While Edward and Tracy didn't necessarily like the last answer, Danielle quickly moved forward. I knew they would enjoy this next section. We were going to get into one of the last steps before we could deploy our model: editing the Essbase properties. When you edit the properties you are telling Essbase how you want the resulting Essbase outline to look. For instance, you can define what kind of application we are deploying (ASO, BSO, XOLAP), what the consolidation operators should be, what is the time dimension, For BSO what dimensions are dense and sparse, how to handle shared members, what transformations, formulas, etc. are needed and much more. It is important to know that as you select different parts of a hierarchy, the screens will show you the relevant properties for the selected component. For example, if you select the dimension name, the dimension properties will display with individual properties grouped into a series of tabs (General, Info, Account Info – for measures dimensions, Formula, Alias, UDAs, and Outline Build):

If you change the selection from a dimension name to one of its children, you see an additional tab for Transformations:

Setting Cube Level Properties

There is a lot to cover in this section, so we will take it slowly and go tab by tab. Remember we've selected hierarchies and pulled them together in our cube schema; from the cube schema, we generated the Essbase model. Now we are going to define the cube specific properties within the Essbase model.

1. Right click on the TBC_SampleModel Essbase model and select Edit Properties. (You can also right click on the working pane that shows the model):

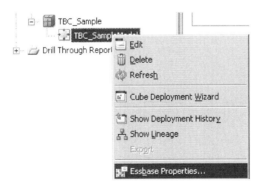

It may take a few moments, but the Properties editor will appear. Notice the screen starts with the Model highlighted and three tabs for General, Alias and Attribute. These are the database level settings:

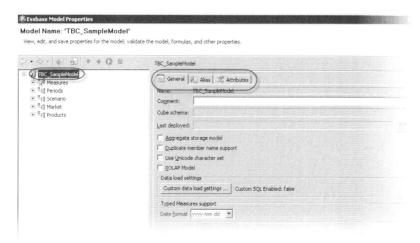

On the General tab, you can define the type of Essbase application as ASO, BSO or XOLAP (Default is BSO), modify the SQL that does the data load and set the date format for typed measures. We will leave everything on the general tab alone for now. We do, however, want to change the order of the dimensions; we want Market to be after Products. We do this using the arrows above the Essbase model. Defining dimension order in the resulting Essbase outline is a new feature in 11.1.2.

2. Click on the dimension Market and click on the down arrow:

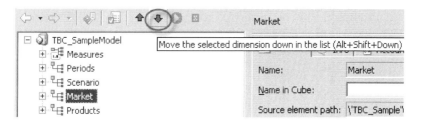

The following message will appear in the right hand pane:

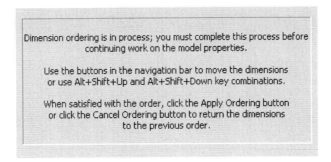

3. Click the Apply changes button to finish the change (or the cancel button to reject it):

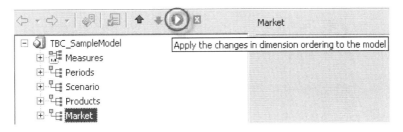

Setting Alias Information

4. Click back on the TBC_SampleModel name and switch to the Alias tab.

Next we need to assign the alias table for the Essbase cube.

5. Highlight the Default Alias table and, using the right arrow, move it into the selected tables box. Notice that if you have multiple alias tables you can reorder them using the up and down arrows:

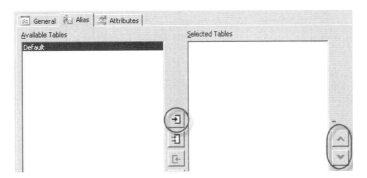

The following alias information only applies to the 11.1.2.2 release and beyond. I mentioned when talking about Alias sets earlier you can have the same names alias set in multiple folders. I also recommended that you don't do this, but if you didn't listen to me and created them, you might have some maintenance to do. If you bring in two alias sets with the same name (but different paths) into the properties, you will get the following error message:

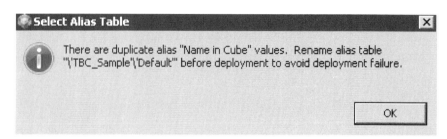

You need to exit out of the Model properties and rename one of the alias sets to make it unique. You will not get this error if you are using unique names for your alias set.

Tip!

In the readme for this release, it says you can use the name in cube feature to rename the duplicate alias set. I was not able to do this, so it is either a bug or the documentation is wrong.

Setting Global Attribute information

6. Select the Attribute tab.

You define the cube level Attribute settings on this tab like defining prefixes for attribute member names or defining the format for date type attributes. We will leave this tab alone for our exercise.

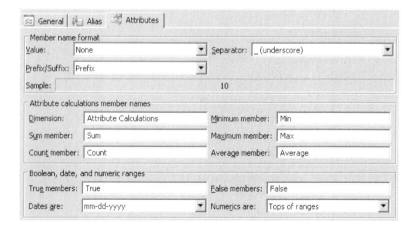

Now that we've set all of the cube level properties, we'll turn our attention to setting dimension level properties.

Setting Dimensional and Column Level Properties

7. Click on the Measures dimension.

Notice that the available tabs are completely different with the Measures hierarchy selected. On the General tab, we can change the name of the dimension as it will appear in the cube, put in a comment and/or assign generation or level names:

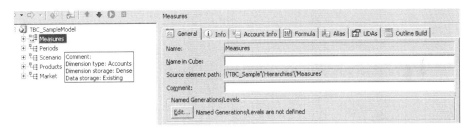

8. Leave defaults for the General tab.
9. Skip over to the Outline Build tab.

On this tab we set Hierarchy setting for ASO cubes, duplicate member settings and data load optimization. In our case, we want to make sure shared members do not get moved(called duplicate members in Studio).

10. Click on Do not move duplicate members.
11. Select Reverse position of shared and actual members if shared member is located before actual member.

This setting is very important in ASO databases; it can also save you grief in BSO databases. In ASO databases, you will get an error in validation if a shared member exists before its stored member. In BSO cubes, you will get a warning, but it will allow you to save the outline. That does not mean everything is ok because you could end up with incorrect totals and calculations in your BSO cube.

12. Click Apply to save what we have done so far:

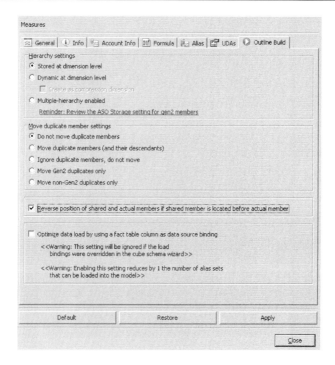

We will want the same Outline build settings for all of our dimensions, so we are going to repeat the steps for the other hierarchies(dimensions) in the Essbase model.

13. Select the Periods member
14. Click on Do not move shared members.
15. Select Reverse position of shared and actual members if shared member is located before actual member.
16. Select the Scenarios member
17. Click on Do not move shared members.
18. Select Reverse position of shared and actual members if shared member is located before actual member.
19. Select the Products member
20. Click on Do not move shared members.
21. Select Reverse position of shared and actual members if shared member is located before actual member.
22. Finally select the Market dimension member
23. Click on Do not move shared members.
24. Select Reverse position of shared and actual members if shared member is located before actual member.
25. Click Apply.

Now we need to set properties for the members within the dimensions.

26. Expand out the Measures dimension and click on the column Child.
27. Click on the Info tab.

Tip!

In Parent/Child hierarchies, we always set the properties on the child and not the parent.

The Info tab is divided into multiple sections: a Consolidations section to define the unary operators, Data Storage section to define member storage properties, Solve Order section to define the solve order for dimensions and members in ASO cubes, and Two Pass section to define two pass settings for BSO members. You can "hard code" values by selecting an option on this screen. For example, if you select the + Consolidation property all members in the dimension will have the + property. That works for some of our sparse dimensions like Entity or Product where members just sum total up the hierarchy. But for our Measures or Accounts dimension this can be problematic. Some members in the accounts dimension will be a "+" consolidation property while others may use the other available properties like "-" or "~" or "^". When properties vary by member, you probably want to consider sourcing the property from a data source that stores this information. We will be using external sources for a number of our properties. External source simply means we are storing the values for the properties in our source. We use the columns from our tables to update the properties. For example in our measures table, we have columns for Consolidation, storage, Variance reporting, Time balance, UDAs and formulas. We can use these values to define the properties in the final cube.

PARENT	CHILD	MEASURES_ALIAS	CONSOLIDATION	TWOPASSCALC	STORAGE	VARIANCEREPORTING	TIMEBALANCE	SKIP	UDA	FORMULA
Measures	Profit		+		X					
Profit	Margin		+		X					
Margin	Sales		+							
Margin	COGS	Cost of Goods Sold	-			E				
Profit	Total Expenses		-		X	E				
Total Expenses	Marketing		+			E				
Total Expenses	Payroll		+			E				
Total Expenses	Misc	Miscellaneous	+			E				
Measures	Inventory		~		O					
Inventory	Opening Inventory		+			E	F			IF(NOT @SMBR...
Inventory	Additions		~			E				
Inventory	Ending Inventory		~			E	L			
Measures	Ratios		~		O					

28. In the Consolidation section, click on External source. Drop down the list and select CONSOLIDATION .
29. In Two_Pass Calculation section, click External source and select TWOPASSCALC.
30. In Data Storage section, click External source and select STORAGE:

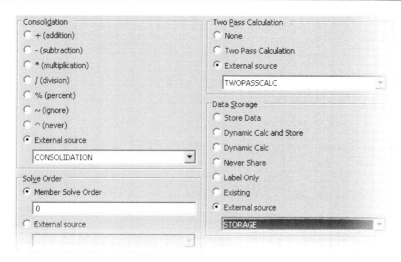

31. Since we are not building an ASO cube, we can ignore the Solve Order section.

32. Switch to the Account Info tab.

This tab is used for account dimension-specific settings. Since we are working in the dimension set as Accounts, we can make changes here. Again in this example we are going to set the options to use External source. Specifically, TIMEBALANCE, SKIP and VARIANCEREPORTING (e.g. some members will be revenue type and others expense type, some members will be a TBLast while others a TBAverage). We could set up options to scale the data here as well, but we won't.

33. In Time Balance section, click External Source and select TIMEBALANCE.

34. In Skip, click External Source and select SKIP.

35. In Variance Reporting section, click External Source and select VARIANCEREPORTING:

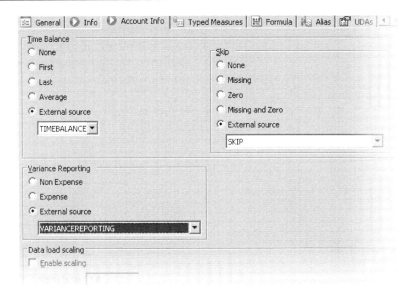

36. Select the Typed Measures tab.

Remember when we created the text measure for Sales_Ranking? Well, here is where we can apply it (note: this tab was not available until 11.1.2). Typed "measures", as the name implies, are only valid in the Accounts dimension.

37. Expand out the tree under TBC_Sample and find the dimensional element called Sales_Ranking.

38. Click on it and it should appear in the Current Assigned Text List box:

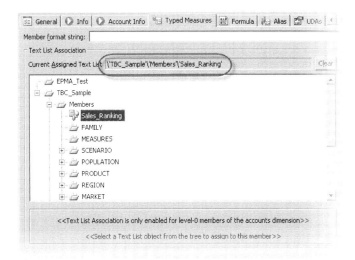

If we wanted to create a member format we would do it on this screen as well, but we won't. For those of you who are intrigued about what a member format is, it is a feature that first appeared in Essbase 11.1.X that uses a MDX expression to reformat the data values in cells so they appear with commas, decimal points or as text. If you really want to learn more about format strings, I suggest you read about formatstrings in *Look Smarter Than You Are With Essbase 11 An Administrators Guide* (page 232 specifically).

39. Moving forward: let's switch to the Formula tab.

If we had user defined members we could apply a formula directly here. For example, for the top of the dimension Products we could put in a formula "East" + "West" + "North" (who cares about south, anyway?). Or, like other settings, we can get the formula from our source. This is what we are going to do.

40. Select External Source and choose the column Formula:

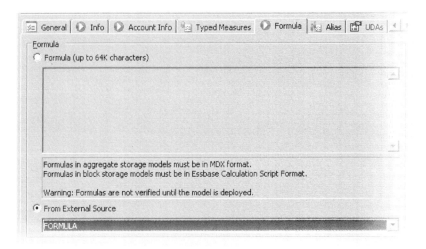

Be aware that you could put anything into a formula. The formula is not validated until it is actually deployed into an Essbase database.

Tip!

Make sure the formula is the correct type for the database type you are creating - MDX for ASO and XOLAP and Calc script language for BSO.

41. Switch to the Alias tab.

On the Alias tab, you will see that the default Alias set is being used in our build. This screen also gives you the ability to create replacement rules for the Alias member in case you need to modify it in any way. We will not be doing anything on this tab.

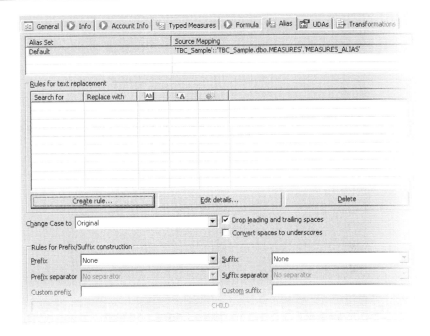

42. Switch to the UDAs tab.

The UDAs tab is where we will define information about UDAs for the selected dimension. Because a member can have multiple UDAs, this tab works a little differently than the other tabs. You define the manual UDA and/or columns that contain UDAs and add them to a list. The list of UDAs gets added to individual members. Let's create both a manual UDA and use an externally sourced UDA.

To add a manual UDA,

43. In the UDA Value box type System_Generated

Now we will add an externally sourced UDA.

44. Click on Add to list button.
45. From the drop down for External source, find and select UDA.
46. Click on Add to list:

This will cause Studio to add the UDA "System_Generated" to every member and whatever the UDA from our source table for the level we have selected.

If we made a mistake or want to remove a UDA from the list, highlight the item and click on the garbage can.

47. Finally, click on the Transformations tab.

Here is where we would add any transformation rules for the member if we had any. For example: we want to change the product family name from Fruit Soda to Fruit Drinks since we added non-carbonated drinks to the line . To add a new transformation

48. Select the member Family from the Products dimension

49. Click on Create rule button

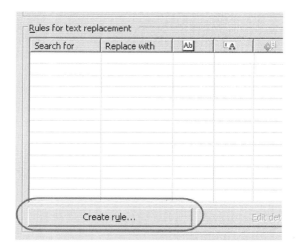

50. A box appears to set up the transformation. In the search for box enter Soda and in the Replace with box enter Drinks

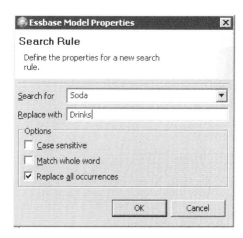

Notice you have options just like in EAS for case sensitivity, Matching whole word and replacing all occurences.

51. Click OK

The replacement is added to the transformations screen. It is possible to change the replacement by highlighting it and clicking on the Edit details button. Similarly, to delete a replacement, highlight it and click on the Delete button.

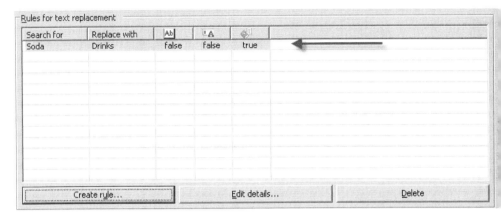

Tip!

If you are doing a transformation on a parent/child file, you will most likely have to do the transformation on both the parent and the child members to make the build work properly.

Appling Changes to Essbase Model

We are done with the Child member of the Measures dimension. At this point I typically have a huge urge to click Close, but we are not done yet. If you have the same urge, click Apply instead to save your changes so far.

Now that you've defined both cube, dimension and member level settings for the Measures dimension, we need to set the properties for the remaining dimensions. How? The steps are the same steps that you performed for the Measures dimension without the Account Info and Typed Measures tabs.

So here's the testing-your-knowledge portion of the book: There are a number of other changes you need to do at this point that are detailed below. I'll give you the dimension member, the change and what tab you should be on to make that change. Go forth, my Studio participants and define the following settings for your cube mode:

Dimension/Member	Change	Tab
Periods/Periods	Specify as the time dimension	Info
	Make Dense	Info
Scenario/Scenario(dimension member)	Set as Label Only	Info
Scenario/Scenario(Child member)	Set external Consolidation as Consolidation	Info
Scenario/Variance	Set consolidation to ~	Info
Scenario/Variance	Optionally, add the formula @VAR("Actual","Budget");	Formula
Scenario/Variance%	Set consolidation to ~	Info
Scenario/Variance%	Optionally, add the formula @VAR%("Actual","Budget");	Formula
Products/Diet Drinks	Set Consolidation to ~	Info

Dynamic Time Series and 11.2.2.2 Alias sets

In the above exercise, we did not enable Dynamic Time Series (DTS). If we are creating a BSO cube we could easily do so by clicking on the DTS button (on the info tab). It works just like setting DTS in a cube managed in EAS.

In 11.1.2.2 this functionality has been enhanced when using multiple Alias sets. Now you can specify different aliases for each set. The screen shot below shows how we turned on the Year to Date member and used different aliases for our different alias sets. After enabling this setting, users can use Y-T-D, YTD or Year_To_Date to retrieve the year to date numbers.

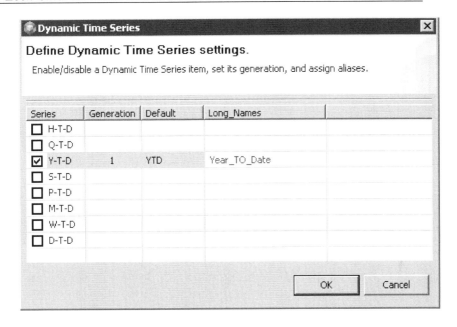

Validating the Essbase Model

If you want to make sure you don't have any problems with the model so far, you can click on the apply button (if available) then on the validate button:

A dialog will appear to show you the issues either as warnings ("hey, here's something you may want to take a look at but you can still try to deploy me") or errors ("Houston, we have a problem. Fix me now."). In the message below, we'll review the warning message and take note. Yes, we understand that our child data storage property is dependent upon valid values being stored in the source table. Since we know the table has valid values (e.g. Store, Dynamic), we'll continue on. In real life, you may want to review the source table and confirm that valid values exist for all members:

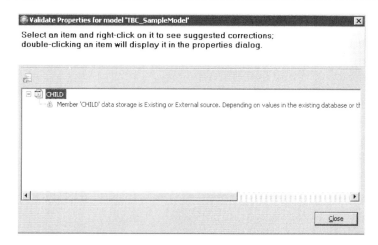

CREATING ATTRIBUTE DIMENSIONS

Tracy was always full of questions, and she had a memory like an elephant. She recalled that when we created the Products hierarchy we added what we thought were attributes dimensions and I told them "I'll be back." Well, I didn't really say that, but I did say we would get to actually defining the attributes once we edited the Essbase properties. Tracy reminded me about this. Well, now is the time to do it. We can create the attributes as regular attribute dimensions or we can create them as varying attributes. Studio is currently the only way to automate the build of varying attributes(They can be manually built from EAS). If we do nothing with the hierarchy, Essbase will treat it as an alternate rollup, which is not exactly what we want.

So let's create a regular attribute dimension!

Creating Attribute Dimensions

Of course, regular attribute dimension seems to be an oxymoron, but in this case I mean an attribute associated to a base dimension that is not varying. Most of us know a cubes can have four kinds of attribute dimensions: String, Numeric, Boolean, and Date. It is also necessary that the source column's data type match the attribute type. When in doubt, use the string type.

To create the attribute dimension,

1. Expand the Products tree by clicking on the plus sign.
2. Select the Ounces hierarchy and switch tabs to the General tab.
3. Check the box Essbase Attribute for "SKU" in the Attribute settings area.
4. Optionally change the Attribute dimension name from Ounces to Fluid Ounces.
5. Drop down the list of attribute types and select Numeric: since this attribute is just numeric values.

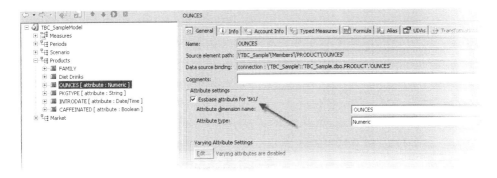

Tip!

If you don't know what kind of data is in your source, the safest attribute type is String.

If you created the hierarchy correctly, the ability to create Ounces as an attribute will be available. If it is not available, go back to the section on Hierarchy creation and correct it. Most likely you did not add SKU as a child of Ounces.

Once it is corrected, you will have to delete and recreate the Essbase model. It seems like a pain, but there are some changes that don't get picked up when you make changes to hierarchies. This is one of those changes.

We are going to repeat these steps to create the other product attribute dimensions.

6. Select the PKGTYPEhierarchy .
7. Check the Attribute check box.
8. Set the attribute type to String attribute type.

9. Select the INTRODATE hierarchy.
10. Check the Attribute check box.
11. Set the attribute type to Date/Time attribute

12. Select the CAFFINATED hierarchy.
13. Check the Attribute check box.
14. Set the attribute type to Boolean attribute type

Remember, if you want to change the generic attribute settings like the member format or attribute calculation names, you can do it by selecting the model name and going to the Attribute tab. These are set at the Essbase model level.

Tip!

Creating Varying Attributes

A varying attribute dimension is a dimension that can change across one or more other dimensions in a BSO database. This new Essbase 11 feature allows you to store data for situations where attributes can change: for example, an employee hierarchy (over time) or a product packaging hierarchy (over different markets). End-users can analyze data based on a current view point or historical point in time (AKA differing perspectives). The dimensions for which an attribute varies are called the independent dimensions. For more information, Danielle encouraged Edward and Tracy to read "Look Smarter Than You Are With Essbase 11" (they gave her a funny look but she continued on, not noticing). In order to show you how to create a varying attribute, we are going to convert the Ounces attribute dimension into a varying attribute based on Periods.

1. Select the Ounces member and click on the Edit button under Varying Attributes:

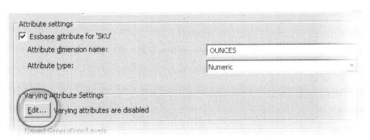

2. In the screen that comes up, check the Create as varying attribute box.
3. Check Periods.

Notice the red circle with the white X in it. If you hover over the X you will get messages about what needs to be done to finish setting up the association. Also notice the options for Association Mode. You have two choices: Keep Existing and Overwrite. Keep Existing will keep the existing values if there are overlapping ranges for an attribute. Overwrite will replace the values with new values.

4. Leave this setting as is:

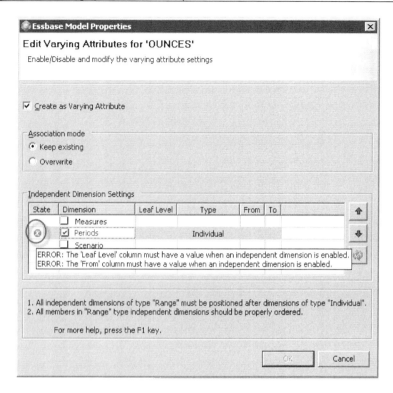

5. In the Leaf level box, double click and select Month as the leaf member (this is the only selection available).
6. Change individual to Range.

Individual is used when the attribute will reflect a discrete value, like a Sales rep for Idaho or Texas. A Range reflects when an attribute is based on a continuum of values like Jan through Mar. The Type Range should be used for date ranges.

7. Double click in the From box and you will get an edit button.

8. Click on the edit button (ellipses):

We will use source data and functions to create the associated member (just like we did when we created the Periods Dimension elements). We will want to use TRANSDATE from the Sales table wrapped in a Month function.

```
'monthShortName'(connection:
\'TBC_Sample'::'TBC_Sample.dbo.SALES'.'TRANSDATE' )
```

We could also add filtering in this step if needed.

9. Type in `'monthShortName'(connection: \'TB:`
`C_Sample'::'TBC_Sample.dbo.SALES'.'TRANSDATE' )`

10. Click OK:

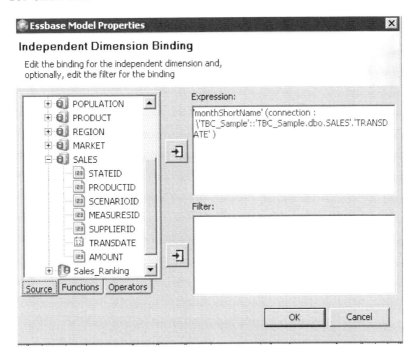

Notice that the white X in the red circle disappeared. This signifies that the minimum requirements for creating the varying attribute were completed:

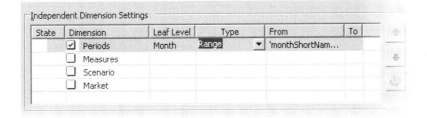

Tip!

If you are using both ranges and individual values, the individual values must occur before the ranges. Studio will rearrange the members for you if you click on the button.

11. Click on the OK button to finish.

How do you tell if you have varying attributes? The only indication is the message next to the Edit button "Varying attributes are enabled".

Since the data isn't really set up to handle varying attributes for our exercise, it is important to go back into Edit and disable the Varying attribute so Ounces is treated as a regular attribute again.

To disable the varying attribute,

1. Click on the Varying Attribute Settings Edit button:

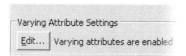

2. In the dialog that appears, uncheck the Create as Varying attribute check box:

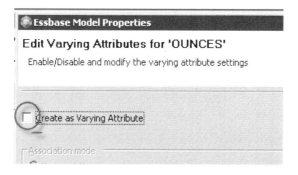

3. Click OK.

OPTIMIZING LOADING DATA

We will go into depth later in the tour about loading data from Studio. But since one of the options available to you when you are editing the Essbase model properties is the ability to optimize your data loads, Danielle thought it important to discuss them while editing the Model properties.

OPTIMIZING DATA LOADS WITH CUSTOM SQL

While Studio will generate the SQL for your data loads, Danielle is quick to point out that there are two ways to optimize that SQL. We won't perform any exercises but if you'd like to follow with the screen shots, you can.

Method 1 – Optimizing Data Load SQL

If the Fact table contains the correct member names for a dimension, there is no need to do a join to the dimension table to get the data. In our case, the Sales table is populated with only key values, but if we were using a table or view that gave us the actual member name like:

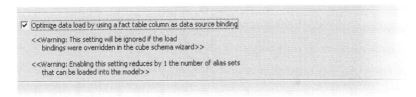

SKU	STATE	SCENARIO	Period	Year	SALES	COGS
100-10	California	Actual	Jan	2000	176.28	70.46
100-10	California	Actual	Jan	2000	501.72	200.54
100-10	California	Budget	Jan	2000	840	340
100-20	California	Actual	Jan	2000	2.36	2.88
100-20	California	Actual	Jan	2000	29.5	36
100-20	California	Budget	Jan	2000	37.8	48.6

We could, by selecting each dimension member and going to the Outline build tab, select to pick up the column from the fact table:

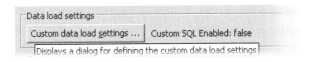

Notice the warning that tuning step reduces the number of alias sets available to be used by one. You have 32 possible Alias sets to use; do you care?

Method 2 – Optimizing Data Load SQL

If you are a good SQL programmer, you can write your own SQL that is more efficient SQL than the Studio generated SQL. To do this, you first select the model name, in our case TBC_Sample. On the General Tab, select the Custom data loads settings button:

Data load settings

| Custom data load settings ... | Custom SQL Enabled: false |

Displays a dialog for defining the custom data load settings

Once in the screen, the generated SQL is shown to you. You have the option to enable Custom SQL and a place to create it. Danielle mentioned a few things about creating your own custom SQL:

- The output columns have to be the same number and order as what Studio generates.
- You should keep the same aliasing and naming that Studio uses. Studio generates a CP_XXX for each table, where XXX is the table ID.
- It is much easier and more practical to copy the system generated SQL into your favorite SQL editor and modify and test it there. The little box that Studio offers is cumbersome to work in:

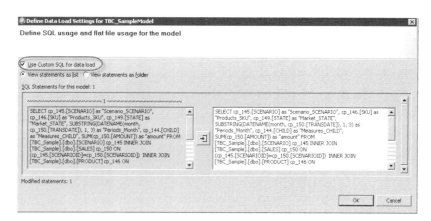

Now that we've set Essbase properties and prepared the Essbase model for data loading, let's complete those last minute Essbase model tasks before deploying it.

FINALIZING THE ESSBASE MODEL

Once you have the changes made to your model, there are a few things you can do.

Viewing Essbase Model Changes

To look at the changes you made to the model, click on the button; it will show you a list by dimension of all of the changes you made in the current editing session. Once you close the properties editor, the list is removed. Something similar to the screen below will appear showing you what was changed:

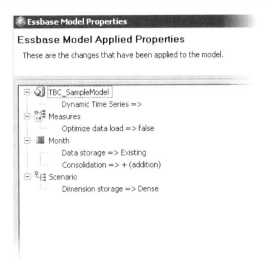

Validating the Essbase Model (Again)

Next we want to validate the model. It is easily done by clicking on the ⬚ button.

12. Click the Validate button.

Warnings and errors may appear. In some cases, these are just warnings and you can let them go. Other times you will find errors that must be fixed before deployment. The yellow triangle with the exclamation point marks a warning and the red circle with the white X marks an error. (I know the book is in black and white; you will have to trust me on the colors):

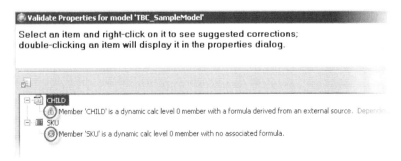

13. Once the cube has validated, click the Close button to close the Editor.

When you click on Close, unless you turned it off, you will see a message:

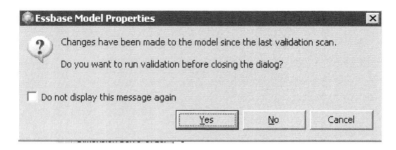

This gives you another opportunity to validate the model for correctness. This is important if you haven't applied changes or validated the model during the session. I recommend clicking Yes and viewing the warnings and errors one more time. If you click on Yes, when it is done, you will have to click on Close once more to actually close the dialog. Of course, if you were brave (foolhardy) you clicked on No, it saved the changes and closed the dialog immediately.

If Tracy and Edward were impressed with Danielle before, they were mesmerized now. Danielle truly was an artist; turning simple hierarchies into what they could tell would be an awesome cube. What was truly amazing to them was the speed at which she was able to do it. This part of the tour took only minutes.

Given a choice, I think both of my visitors would have stayed with Danielle all day; Edward was digging deep into his pockets to get quarters out, but all he found was a flyer for the Spinning Beaver Lodge, and Danielle did not flip over it. Edward said this was an inside joke and you would have to get him drunk to tell it. Do vegans drink alcohol? Beer is just hops and grains! It was time to move on before the PC police arrived. We were going to where we could actually see the fruits of our labor: the Distribution Department where Essbase models were deployed to an actual Essbase cube.

Chapter 9:
Distribution

The tram took us through the set of Nightmare on Implementation Street with star Eddy Krueger before heading on to Distribution. I thought it was serendipitous as Essbase Studio makes implementations easy. We arrived at Distribution in a jiffy.

"You realize that a jiffy is the time it takes for light to travel one centimeter in a vacuum?"

I turned my head and there he was: Other Ed. I don't know how he knew I was thinking about the word jiffy.

"Yeah, it's also the name of a peanut butter," I quickly responded, not to be outdone.

Other Ed is our guru in charge of distribution. It's the perfect job for him. He acts slowly, but seems to get results almost magically. The things locked in his brain often amazed me.

I introduced Other Ed to Edward and they had an immediate bond. It seemed like Ed was Edward's brother from another mother, his soul mate. This scared both Tracy and me. The two interacted like they read each other's minds.

As we were pondering this, without prompting, Other Ed starting talking about what goes on in Distribution. "Edward, Tracy, Distribution is where we take the Essbase models and deploy them to Essbase."

I started to interject with a metaphor but Other Ed beat me to it. "Yes, it is like deploying troops; we have a lot of options of where, when and how they are sent out. You can deploy just the outlines, or outlines and data in a number of different ways. You can deploy to one server or many different servers from the same Studio instance. Follow me now and I'll show you how."

DEPLOYING AN ESSBASE MODEL

Other Ed didn't hesitate as he jumped into the steps of Essbase deployment.

To deploy an Essbase model to the Essbase server,

1. In the Essbase Studio Metadata Navigator, highlight the Essbase model TBC_SampleModel.
2. Right click on it and select Cube Deployment Wizard (not the Harry Potter Wizard option):

If this is the first time you are deploying, you may need to set up a connection to an Essbase server. If the following screen appears, enter in the server information including a name for the connection, Server, ID and password. If this is a clustered server, check the cluster box. Click Login:

A wizard will appear. If you chose the Harry Potter Wizard, at this point you are seeing a gangly boy with glasses and a strange lightning scar on his forehead. Go back and start over, selecting the Cube Deployment Wizard.

The Cube Deployment Wizard is powerful with many magical features: it contains the list of your Essbase connections, provides the ability to create a new connection, specifies how you want to connect to your data source and allows the editing of the Essbase model properties. From the application dropdown, you will see the list of existing Essbase applications for the selected Essbase server. You can either select one of these or type in a new application name. My example uses a new database called TBC with a database named Sample.

Tip!

Once you create a connection to Essbase it shows up in the Data source connections and is reusable.

3. If you don't see your Essbase server in the drop down list for Essbase Server Connection, select the New Connection button.
4. Enter the Essbase server information (Connection name, Description, Server name or IP, port – default is 1423, Essbase administrator user id and password):

5. Click OK.
6. Select your Essbase Server from the Essbase Server Connection (hopefully this is your development or test server).
7. Type in "TBC" for Application.
8. Type "Sample" for Database:

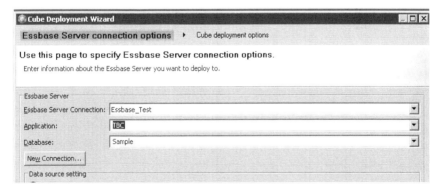

If you are using Studio 11.1.2.2 you have a new deployment option to enable streaming mode. Streaming mode determines how connectivity will be handled. In non-streaming mode Essbase talks to the ODBC or OCI connection directly. In streaming mode, the communication is handled by on the Studio server. Non-streaming mode is faster but requires the ODBC connections be set up on the Essbase server the same as on the Studio server.

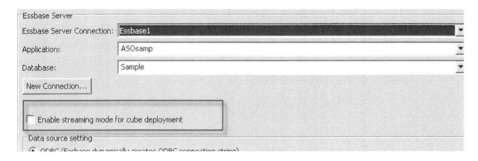

Next, we select the Data source setting. By default it generates a string for you, but you can override it by supplying a different ODBC connection to use or in the case of an Oracle relational database source, use the quicker OCI connection identifier.

9. We will use the default setting so leave ODBC (Essbase dynamically creates ODBC connection string):

Data source setting

⊙ ODBC (Essbase dynamically creates ODBC connection string)

○ ODBC (Enter ODBC DSN name) [   ]

○ OCI (Enter OCI connect identifier) [   ]

---

10. Click on Next to get to the next screen.

The next screen allows you to specify what kind of load task to do. You can just build the outline, just load data, or do both. If you load data or do both, you can specify how the data load works.

11. For now, since this is the first time we are building the outline, we will Build Outline only:

Load task type
⊙ Build outline
○ Load data
○ Build outline and load data

Load data options
⊙ Add to existing data
○ Subtract from existing data
○ Overwrite existing data

This will give us a chance to make sure the model works like we want it to before we load the data.

When we select Build Outline only, we have a number of other options to select as shown in the screen below:

☐ Delete all members first
☐ Delete and restore database
☐ Incremental load
☐ Create and save rule file only

- Delete all members first deletes all the members in hierarchies.
- Delete and restore database completely deletes the database.
- Incremental load allows for selective updating of dimensions (which allows us another screen to play with).
- Create and save rule file only does not do the actual load but just creates the load rules for us for future use.

12. For our load right now, select Incremental Load.

Next, we select how to deal with rejected records and how the process will be run. Within the rejected records section, you have a number of options to select. First, you select the number of rejected records to keep. By default Studio keeps all rejected records, but you can change that to the specific number of rejection rows you want.

Second, you choose where those records are going to go. It goes to the Studio default location. You can change that as well to a location of your choosing.

Finally if you are doing data loads, you can elect to stop loading when the load encounters an error, by default, it continues loading data.

Rejected records settings

Number of records to keep: ⦿ All   ○ Limit   [200]

Error file name: ⦿ Default   ○ File name   [   ]

☐ Stop the data load when the first record is rejected

We will elect to show all error records to the default error location.

13. Choose the option to show All error records and log them to the default location:

Rejected records settings
Number of records to keep: ⊙ All   ○ Limit   [200]
Error file name: ⊙ Default ○ File name [   ]
☐ Stop the data load when the first record is rejected

Scheduling Options
☑ Deploy now
☐ Save as MaxL load script
  File name: [   ] [Browse...]

(?)   < Back   Next >   Finish   Cancel

One of the nice things Studio will do is create the Deploy statement for us for later use. For those who are MaxL challenged like me, it makes life easier.

14. Check the option Save as MaxL load script.
15. Browse and enter a path and script file name.

You must select a location for the file name. Studio will not allow you to click on Next or Finish otherwise

Tip!

16. Click Next.

This screen allows you to select the dimensions to update, the type of update to do and how to deal with existing data in the cube. If you select Update All hierarchies, Studio does an update to all hierarchies. If you select Update or Rebuild selected Hierarchies, the buttons for Update and rebuild are available.

The Update option adds new members to a hierarchy and will do reorganizations of members based on source data. When you click on a dimension and select Update a blue arrow appears showing the dimension and columns to be updated:

The Rebuild option deletes the hierarchy then rebuilds it. This is good if you have shared rollups that can change. If we just updated the hierarchy, shared members would not get removed from their old parent. When you select Rebuild, a red X appears signifying the dimension will be deleted and rebuilt:

Since this is the first time we are building our outline, we'll update all hierarchies.

17. Select Update all hierarchies:

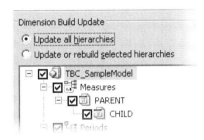

Finally, we need to deal with what we want to do with existing data in the cube. Again, since this is our first time building the cube and there is no data, it really does not matter what we choose. If there were data in the cube, just like from EAS we could choose to keep all existing data, keep just the input data, keep only level 0 data or get rid of any data (No data).

18. Choose No Data.
19. To actually build the cube click on Finish:

Since the cube has never been built before, it is foolish that I chose to do an incremental build. If this is the first deployment to this cube, you may get the following message. If so, just click on Yes to build the Essbase cube:

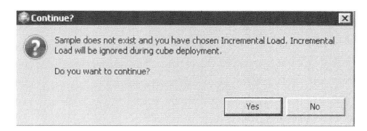

A screen will appear to show us the status of the build process. It will show you if the build was successful or if there were errors. It is important to look through this screen:

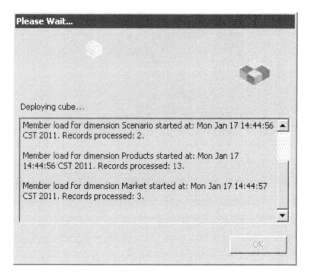

20. Review the messages from deployment (hopefully you see the following "successful" message:

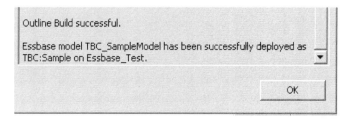

21. Click OK after reviewing the messages.

Tip!

If there were errors, the cube most likely did not deploy; look at the errors and determine the problem. Even if the cube deployed, you can still have errors in error files; for example, a member did not load. Remember to check these out.

Viewing the Deployed Essbase Cube

"Now that we successfully deployed our cube, let's see what it looks like," Other Ed said giddily. "If EAS and Studio are installed on the same server and it is configured, we can launch EAS from Studio. Just go to Tools>>Launch Essbase Administration Services Console." If not, launch your EAS Console the old fashioned way (either Start >> Programs >>... or from the web url).

1. Select Tools>>Launch Essbase Administration Services Console:

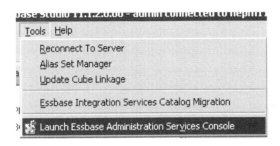

2. Expand the Essbase server >> Applications. You should see a new application called TBC.
3. Expand TBC and you should see the new database, Sample.
4. Expand Sample and then Rules Files.

The Cube Deployment Wizard created a number of rules files for building the outline, in some cases multiple ones for a dimension:

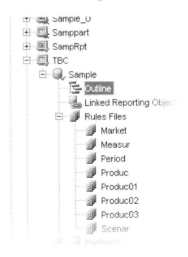

Now let's edit one of them.

5. Right click on the Market Rules file and select Edit.

Notice the message box that appears (that will appear whether you have the rules file locked or not):

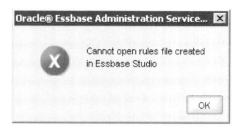

You can't edit dimension rules files created in Studio from EAS.

6. Double click on the Sample outline to open the outline. You should see something like the following (magic):

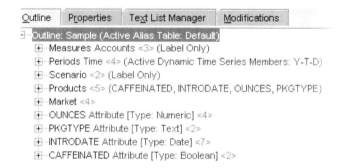

Tip!

Your build may not look exactly like mine. For example, In my screen, I had not changed ounces to Fluid Ounces and I did not include variances in my Scenario dimension.

Review the dimensions and members built by Essbase Studio. Do they have aliases, UDAs, Formulas, and all of the expected Essbase properties?

7. Click Verify to validate the outline.

Did you get an error message? You should have! The sample data does not have the formula in opening inventory correct. If you want to correct it, put double quotes around the names Opening Inventory and Closing Inventory so they are recognized as members with spaces in the names. This error occurs because the quotes in the formula names get stripped off during load. To correct this, in the source table you would need to have a backslash in front of every quote as an escape character. Like \"Opening Inventory\"

If you see things in the Cube you don't like, go back to the model and see if you can figure out how to change them. For instance, if you did not sort the time dimension, add a sort of transdate to get them in the right order.

LOADING DATA

"Now that we have successfully built an outline and it was quick and pretty painless except for Edward hitting me with that stupid light saber," Other Ed continued, "we will now load data. The process is simpler than building the outline."

1. Right click on the Model and select Cube deployment Wizard (just like before).
2. In the application dropdown, select the TBC application. It should select the Sample database automatically.
3. Click Next.

Tip!

The Application always reverts back to the first application on the server. Make sure you select your application every time.

4. Select Load Data and click, add to existing Values and click on Finish:

5. You will get the following message. Just click on Yes (we haven't loaded any data yet so no reason to choose Incremental):

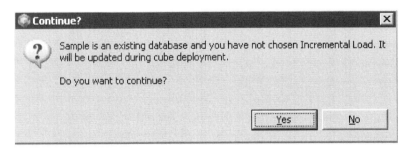

When the deployment is done, you should see the following screen showing you how many rows were loaded, if there were errors and the status of the load process:

6. Click OK.
7. Open Excel and from Smart View, connect to your server and retrieve data from your newly loaded TBC database.
   You will most likely see:

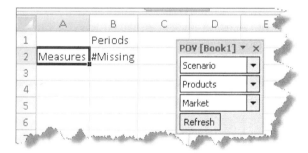

This is because while Studio loaded the data, it did not run any calculations to aggregate it. From Smart View or the EAS Console, run the default calculation:

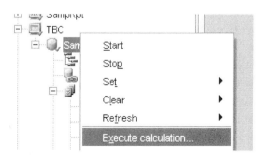

8. Now try to retrieve data. If you so desire, you can also zoom in and pivot to explore the cube:

	A	B	C	D	E
1		Jan	Feb	Mar	Apr
2	Sales	31538	32069	32213	3291
3	Cost of Goods Sold	14160	14307		14675
4	Marketing	5223	5289		542
5	Payroll	4056	4056		40
6	Miscellaneous	75	71		96
7	Opening Inventory	117405	116434		11914
8	Additions	30567	31193		39657
9	Ending Inventory	116434	115558	119143	12588
10	Margin %	55.10178198	55.38682216	55.26650731	55.418177

POV [Book1] × — Scenario — Products — Market — Refresh

Other Ed was amused at how shocked Edward and Tracy were at the ease of cube deployment. But Tracy, of course, also wanted to know more. (I swear she wants this book to be 900 pages.) She wanted to know what the button to save the MaxL does. This was no problem for our deployment specialist. He decided he would give them the most options by loading both the outline and data and doing an incremental build of the database.

BUILDING A DEPLOYMENT MAXL

OE (Other Ed - I got tired of typing Other Ed and he is, after all, a Hollywood type) explained to Tracy that the option she was asking about helps make automation easier. First select the deployment options in the wizard desired. Then specify that the wizard should save the MaxL. Finally when you click on finish, a deploy statement is generated in the proper format for MaxL into a text file. This statement can be used in any MaxL script you like.

One of the nice things about deployment is it allows you to do incremental builds of your applications. You can select two different types of dimension changes. You can do updates or rebuilds of dimensions. With an update, the new members are added to the dimension. With Rebuild, the members within the dimension are deleted and re-added. This is very helpful if you have shared member hierarchies that have members that move from parent to parent. Rebuilding the dimension allows these shared members to get moved to the proper parent without getting duplicated.

To build a deployment MaxL script,

1. Select the TBC_SampleModel and, like before, right click and start up the deployment wizard.
2. Select the TBC application and Database and click Next.

With the load task types you can just build the outline, just load data or do both.

3. Select Build outline and load data.

We also have to decide how deal with data being added. Should it be added to existing data, subtracted from it or overwrite data. We will overwrite it.

4. Overwrite existing data.

When building the outline, you have a number of choices. You can:

*   Delete all the members in the outline before you build.
*   Delete the entire database and recreate it.
*   Do an incremental load. This allows you to specify dimensions to update, how to update them and what to do with existing data in the cube.

5. Check Incremental load to select it. (The Next button is not available if you do not check this box)

Finally we can have the deployment wizard just create dimension build and data load rules for use later.

In the scheduling section, we can have the deploy run when we click on Finish or we can just create the deploy command to be used later. We are just trying to create a deploy command so:

6. Uncheck Deploy now
7. Check Save as MaxL load Script.
8. Click on Browse, find a location to store the file and name it.
9. Click on Next:

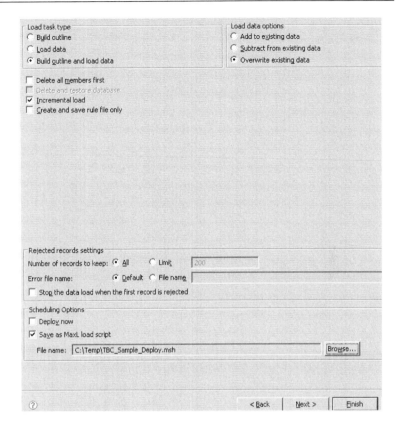

When doing incremental builds, we can do either update or rebuild hierarchies as described above. We will rebuild some dimensions and update others.

10. Select Update or Rebuild Selected Hierarchies.

11. Check the Measures dimension and click on Update.

12. Select the Products Dimension and click on Rebuild.

13. Select the Market Dimension and click on Update.

In our case, our cube does not have any data in it, but if it did, we could save different amount of data, from none to just level zero, to input data to all data.

14. In the Preserve dropdown, select No Data:

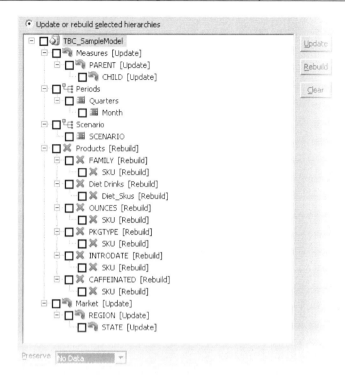

15. Click Finish. You will see the following (with your path and file name of course):

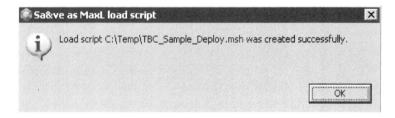

16. Navigate the file system to where you stored the file and open it with Notepad.
    You should see something like:

```
deploy all from model 'TBC_SampleModel' in cube
schema '\TBC_Sample\Cube Schemas\TBC_Sample' with
option delete_members using incremental_load modify
using update for 'Measures'-<'PARENT'-<'CHILD',
rebuild for 'Products', update for 'Market'-
<'REGION'-<'STATE' preserve no data login $1
identified by $2 on host 'nepm1112' to application
```

> 'TBC' database 'Sample' add values using connection
> 'Essbase_Test' keep all errors on error ignore
> dataload write to default;

You can now use this command in any MaxL script. If you want to deploy with different options, you can either rerun the wizard or you can modify the generated command. The syntax is available in the Essbase Tech reference.

Other Ed was beaming; he showed the dynamic duo how they could create the automation for their cube in less than 2 minutes.

"Essbase Studio even uses variables for the login parameters. Of course, this script could also easily be encrypted using MaxL encryption commands, but it is outside the realm of Other Ed to tell you," said Other Ed. Funny how he talks sometimes, referring to himself in the third person.

DEPLOYMENT HISTORY

Our mystical magical tour of deployment was not quite over. OE had one more thing to show us. Not only can you deploy the Essbase model to one or more servers, to one or more applications, or to one or more databases, you can also see the results of any of those deployments.

1. In Essbase Studio, expan-d the TBC_Sample cube schema and TBC_SampleModel Essbase model.
2. You should see the newly deployed Essbase cube, TBC.Sample:

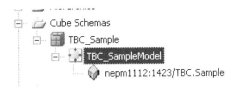

That was cool in itself, but then OE showed something even more spectacular.

3. Right click on the Essbase model, TBC_SampleModel and select Show Deployment History:

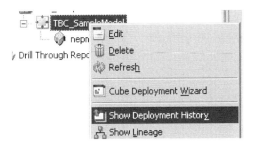

You can track every deployment of the model!

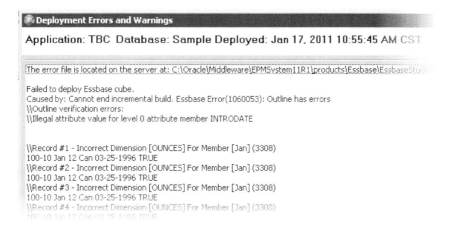

If you notice, in the first row, OE created a failure row just to show what it looks like. He showed Tracy (since Edward was off in his own world somewhere) that by clicking on the failed status you are able to see information about the deployment issues:

Deployment Errors and Warnings

Application: TBC Database: Sample Deployed: Jan 17, 2011 10:55:45 AM CST

The error file is located on the server at: C:\Oracle\Middleware\EPMSystem11R1\products\Essbase\EssbaseStu

Failed to deploy Essbase cube.
Caused by: Cannot end incremental build. Essbase Error(1060053): Outline has errors
\\Outline verification errors:
\\Illegal attribute value for level 0 attribute member INTRODATE

\\Record #1 - Incorrect Dimension [OUNCES] For Member [Jan] (3308)
100-10 Jan 12 Can 03-25-1996 TRUE
\\Record #2 - Incorrect Dimension [OUNCES] For Member [Jan] (3308)
100-10 Jan 12 Can 03-25-1996 TRUE
\\Record #3 - Incorrect Dimension [OUNCES] For Member [Jan] (3308)
100-10 Jan 12 Can 03-25-1996 TRUE
\\Record #4 - Incorrect Dimension [OUNCES] For Member [Jan] (3308)
100-10 Jan 12 Can 03-25-1996 TRUE

Since we know you won't have any problems deploying your cubes, you will most likely not have failures to explore. Right! At least, if you followed along in the book properly you won't have errors for this exercise.

Other Ed was truly magical with his Cube Deployment Wizard (way better than Harry Potter and Gandalf). He took the Essbase model and miraculously turned it into an Essbase database in mere minutes. As he often does, Other Ed left Edward and Tracy with something to ponder.

"Your lineage is yet to come," he said mysteriously, walking away providing no chance for further questions.

Edward and Tracy had no idea what he meant but they would before the end of the next chapter.

Well, it was time to get back on the tram and explore more of the Studio. Now that we had successfully deployed a cube, I decided it was a good time to have a little fun. What self-respecting studio tour would not have a theme park attached to it in order to get tourists to spend their last dime? Well we are not self-respecting, but we do have a theme park. It had all the latest rides and cool shows as well. I figured Edward and Tracy would really enjoy the stunt show. At the mention of this Tracy was sent all atwitter (and no, I don't mean she was tweeting). Off to the theme park we go!

CHAPTER 10:
THE STUNT SHOW

"A stunt show?" Edward queried. "How does this relate to the work of Studio?" Ah, the young, impatient type, I thought. Okay. I had to explain it to him even though I knew he wasn't listening to the answer. At our stunt show we do death-defying feats. The main one - and the one being showcased today - was Drill Through. Drill Through is the ability to get data from external sources. Since most data in Essbase is summarized and numeric based, Drill Through allows you to get more detailed and text based information from within your Excel spreadsheet and from other products. For example: retrieving journal lines that make up balances in a P&L or the address and contact information for customers. These Drill Through reports are done from predefined sources. If that is not a stunt, I don't know what is.

Before the show began I explained that there are three types of Drill Through available:

- Relational
- URLs, including FDM and OBI
- Custom Java method

Drill-through to flat file sources is not supported.

Tip!

Today's show concentrated on the first two type of Drill Through, Relational and URLs. Tracy, as always, had a question. She wanted to know why Studio Drill Through was better than what she could get from EIS. It was a good question but simple to answer, which is good because I can't answer hard questions. I quickly explained the following points:

- With Studio, Drill Through is created as a generic query for a data source and then associated to one or more Essbase models. With EIS, Drill Through is cube specific and you have to recreate it every time you want to use it again.
- When you associate a model to a Drill Through report in Studio it associates from shared services. With EIS, you have to rebuild the outline to associate the Drill Through points.
- Studio allows you to drill through on members while EIS does not.
- Studio is a word and not an acronym.
- You can test Studio reports from within Studio. With EIS you have to deploy them, which is much harder to debug.

While pleased with the answer, the unquenchable Tracy asked, "Can I use Drill Through reports with both Smart View and the Classic Add-in?"

I pondered how to respond to this for a minute and decided to answer truthfully. "Yes, of course you can."

I guess I have a mindset like a sales referee (and not an sales representative; no offense sales reps). I couldn't withhold information from them, so I expanded on my answer. Yes, you can use both Smart View and the Classic add-in for Drill Through, but Studio Drill Through is really optimized for Smart View. The visual cues and ease of Drill Through make it easy to get reports. While the Classic add-in can be used for Drill Through, there are a number of requirements and limitations:

- Users must be provisioned in Shared Services.
- Localization is not supported (you cannot drill-through to non-English sources)
- Most importantly, there are no visual cues displayed to show that drill-through is available for an intersection. You just have to "know".
- If you go into the linked object browser, you will see the drill-through report(s) even if they are not valid for the intersection. Only after launching the report will you get a message that there is not a report available for the intersection.

Before Tracy could ask, I continued. There are a couple of caveats you should be aware of if you want to use Drill Through reports.

- For Drill Through to be active, the Studio service has to be running.
- You cannot drill through from HSgetValue formulas, BUT for every HSgetValue on a sheet, Smartview will check with Studio to see if a report is available. This can impact performance tremendously.
- Oracle does not recommend using drill-through with outlines that support duplicate member names, since Studio generates special tags to identify duplicate members.
- When drilling to a URL the URL has to be less than 256 characters long.
- You cannot drill through to EPMA.
- Users must be provisioned in Shared Services.
- If you make a change to a Drill-through report and save it, the changes are immediate. You do not need to wait for any type of refresh.

Now that I had given the introduction and killed a little time it was time for the show to start. The anticipation in the theater arena could be felt by all. I just had to remember not to volunteer if they asked. Last time I was at a stunt show and helped out, I couldn't walk for a week.

CREATING A RELATIONAL DRILL THROUGH REPORT

Silence and tension filled the air as the stunt show started.

1. With Drill Through Reports folder highlighted, right click and select New>>Drill-Through Report:

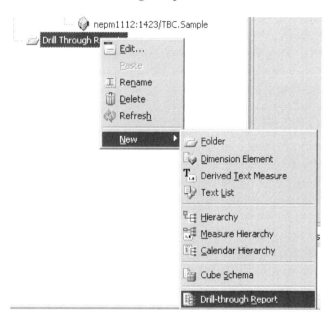

Give the report a meaningful name, I like Suppliers. If desired, put in a comment about the report for people who have to maintain this later so they have a clue about what you did.

2. Type in Suppliers:

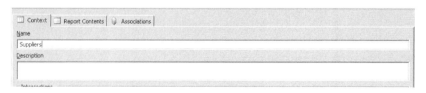

3. Click on the [Add] button to set the hierarchies that will be used in the drill through report.
4. Select the Products ,Measures and Periods.
5. Click OK:

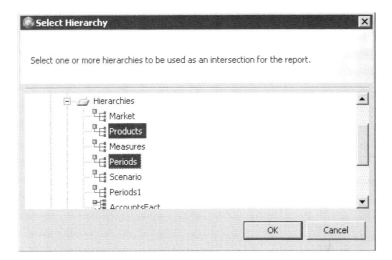

The Dimensions and Hierarchies are brought into the Intersections box. This is where we select at what level the user needs to be in the hierarchy in order to be able to trigger a drill-through report. We only want the user to drill-through if they are at the SKU and Month levels (not Quarter or Family).

6. Uncheck Products and Periods and just put check marks next to the first instance of SKU and at Month:

Tip!

By not including the Attribute dimension members, we have turned off drill-through if attributes are on the worksheet. Make sure to select the attributes if you want to allow drill-through with attributes.

Remember that Measures is a recursive Hierarchy? We need to select members from it in a different way.

7. Click on the Advanced Settings button:

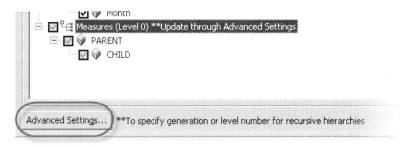

In the screen that appears, for each recursive hierarchy you have (we only have selected one) define whether this is based on generations or levels and what level number it should go to. For our case, we want to use levels and go to up to level 1.

8. Select Level and the number 1.
9. Click OK:

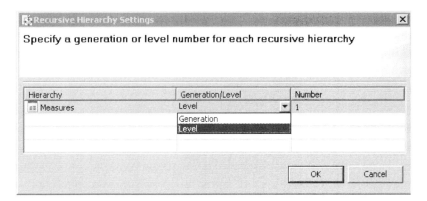

We actually don't want Measures to be a selection in the report, so remove it from the intersections list. Removing an item couldn't be simpler.

10. Highlight the measures dimension
11. Click on the little trashcan button on the right hand side of the screen.

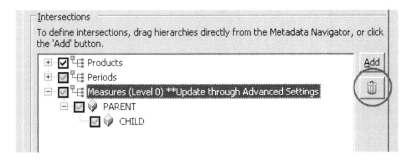

Congratulations! You've just defined the Context (or how the drill through can take place.

Defining Report Contents

12. Next, click on the Report Contents Tab:

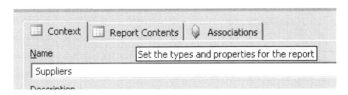

In this tab, you define what kind of drill-through report you want and the columns to be included in report output. This screen is also the starting point to modify the SQL used for drill through, to filter the report and to verify the report results.

13. Select Relational for report drill-through type:

14. Click on the Add button to select what columns will appear on the report.
15. In the Select Column screen that appears, select all of the columns from the Supplier table and scroll down and select the State column from the Market table.
16. Click OK:

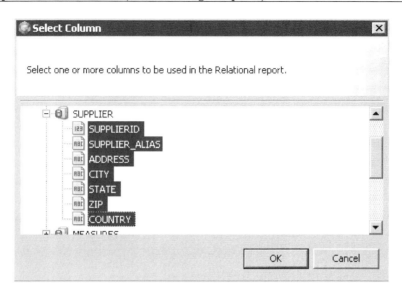

The columns will be added to the Columns Box on the screen. If you want to change the order of the columns, use the up and down arrows. The screen also allows you to aggregate numeric (Sum, min, max, Avg, count) or count non numeric columns. It also lets you sort by columns. We want to sort by SupplierID Ascending, so select that.

17. Select SUPPLIERID and choose a sort order of Asc:

Columns	Display Name	Aggregate	Sort Order
'TBC_Sample.dbo.SUPPLIER'.'SUPPLIERID'	SUPPLIERID		Asc
'TBC_Sample.dbo.SUPPLIER'.'SUPPLIER_ALIAS'	SUPPLIER_ALIAS		
'TBC_Sample.dbo.SUPPLIER'.'ADDRESS'	ADDRESS		
'TBC_Sample.dbo.SUPPLIER'.'CITY'	CITY		
'TBC_Sample.dbo.SUPPLIER'.'STATE'	STATE_1		
'TBC_Sample.dbo.SUPPLIER'.'ZIP'	ZIP		
'TBC_Sample.dbo.SUPPLIER'.'COUNTRY'	COUNTRY		
'TBC_Sample.dbo.PRODUCT'.'SKU'	SKU		
'TBC_Sample.dbo.PRODUCT'.'SKU_ALIAS'	SKU_ALIAS		
'TBC_Sample.dbo.MARKET'.'STATE'	STATE		

Next, we only want unique rows to be returned from our Query, so uncheck Show duplicate records in report.

18. Uncheck the option Show duplicate records in report:

For some strange reason, we only want Markets that are in a state that begins with the letter C (mainly to illustrate how the filter feature in drill through reports work).

19. Click the Filter button:

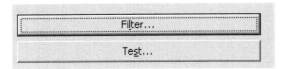

20. Add a filter using functions and the State column from Supplier. The Filter expression should look like:
```
LeftStr(connection :
\'TBC_Sample'::'TBC_Sample.dbo.MARKET'.'STATE',1)
=="C"
```

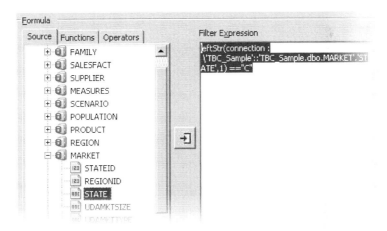

21. Click OK after you enter the expression. If you had an issue with the syntax, you will get a message:

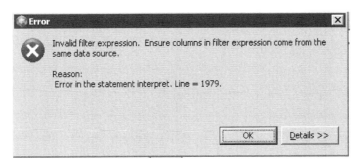

22. Correct errors (make sure it looks like my statement above) and then click OK.
    It is now time to test the query.
23. Click on the Test button.

24. In the screen that appears enter 100-10 for the SKU, Jan for the Month and Sales for the Measures.
25. Click Show Result.

The result set will appear below. You can change the number of rows to display:

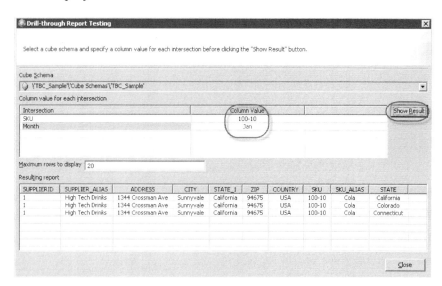

26. Close the preview dialog.

Defining Associations

We will deal with custom SQL later, so for now, click on the associations tab. Here is where you associate the drill-through report to one or more Essbase models (remember, a model can spawn multiple cubes).

27. Check the option to associate the drill-through to TBC_SampleModel:

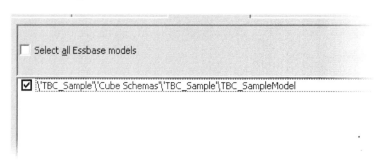

28. Click on Save.

29. Click Save then click Close. The report will be added to the Drill-Through list.

Now that we've created the Drill Through report, we reach the heart stopping part of the stunt show. We'll see the Drill Through report in action!

30. Open Excel and the Smart View Add-in.
31. Log in if necessary and connect to the TBC.Sample database.
32. Edit the Smart View options and enable the Drill-through styles and set a color. I like light yellow:

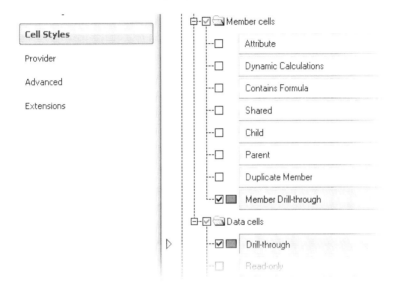

33. If you are using Version 11.1.2.1.103 or higher, change to the advanced tab. Check the box "Display Drill Through Options". This allows you to see the tool tip bubbles notifying you that you have a drill through report available.

If you are not using Drill though, turning off Display Drill Through Options can speed up retrievals.

Tip!

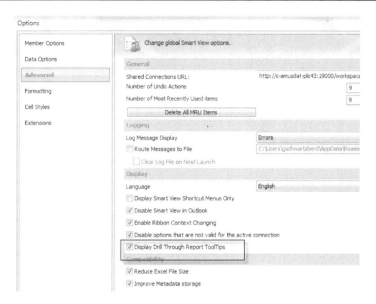

34. Now drill into products until you get to SKU level and Month level.

Notice that the cells have changed color. If you click on a cell you also get a cue that tells you what report(s) is/are available:

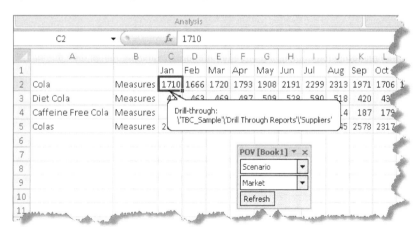

35. Select the Jan/Cola cell. Depending on the version of Smart View you are on, either click on the drill-through button on the Essbase ribbon bar, or right click and select Hyperion>>Drill-Through. The drill-through report will appear on a separate sheet:

	A	B	C	D	E	F	G	H	I	J
1	SUPPLIERID	SUPPLIER_ALIAS	ADDRESS	CITY	STATE_1	ZIP	COUNTRY	SKU	SKU_ALIAS	STATE
2	1	High Tech Drinks	1344 Crossman Ave	Sunnyvale	California	94675	USA	100-10	Cola	California
3	1	High Tech Drinks	1344 Crossman Ave	Sunnyvale	California	94675	USA	100-10	Cola	Colorado
4	1	High Tech Drinks	1344 Crossman Ave	Sunnyvale	California	94675	USA	100-10	Cola	Connectic

"Did you just see that!?!" Edward yelled. "Wow, I never really thought that would be able to work."

CREATING USER DEFINED SQL FOR DRILL-THROUGH

Here is the plot of our next Stunt Show scene: our hero is handcuffed to a bomb with the time showing 12 seconds left and the evil mole people are in the next cave laughing and downing massive amounts of Juju elixir in early celebration of his demise. How does our fearless hero escape? He of course notices that the walls of the cave around him have a deposit of iron ore and he uses it to short out the electronics on the bomb. What does this have to do with User defined SQL? Just like our hero is resourceful and thinks outside the box, User defined SQL allows you to be resourceful and customize your own drill through SQL, overriding the Studio generated SQL (I guess this is why it is called user defined). In many cases, User Defined SQL can be more efficient than generated SQL because you, the developer, know more about the data and table structures than Essbase Studio does. It is just like our hero who knew more than the Mole creatures. While defining user defined SQL is pretty easy, there are some things you need to know in order to make it work properly.

- The columns being returned should be the same and in the same order as what you defined on the reports contents tab.
- Based on the Hierarchies selected, Studio uses a $$Hierarchy-COLUMN$$ nomenclature to return the column name that created a column and $$Hierarchy-VALUE$$ to return the value from the spreadsheet.
- Associated with the last point: when $$Hierarchy_Column$$ is returned it is in the format of CP_XXX, where XXX is the table identified for the table being used. Because of this, it is important to use the same alias names as Studio uses.
- It is easier to copy the SQL out to your favorite SQL editor and make the changes and test it there first (hard coding values) before testing it in the SQL BOX in Studio.

To see what the generation of SQL looks like, look in the log. It will not show you the actual SQL, but will show you what values are being used. For example, the following shows you that for the column SKU the value 100-10 is used and for Month Jan is returned.

```
[SRC_CLASS:
com.hyperion.cp.vm.VmStatementPrimitive]
[SRC_METHOD: runSayStatement] run DTR name: form :
\'TBC_Sample'\'Drill Through Reports'\'test'; args:
hierarchy : \'TBC_Sample'\'Hierarchies'\'Products'
:: class : \'TBC_Sample'\'Members'\'PRODUCT'\'SKU'
:: "100-10", hierarchy :
\'TBC_Sample'\'Hierarchies'\'Periods' :: class :
\'TBC_Sample'\'Members'\'Periods'\'Month' :: "Jan"
```

With these things in mind, let's explore how to create custom SQL.

1. Edit the drill-through report we just created, Suppliers (double click on it or right click and select Edit).
2. Switch to the Report Contents tab.
3. Click on the button Template SQL:

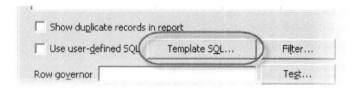

4. Click on the button Get Standard SQL:

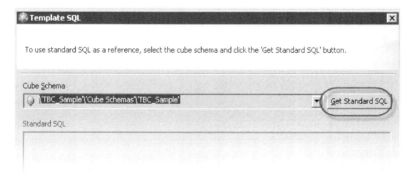

5. The SQL will populate both the Standard SQL box and the User-Defined Box:

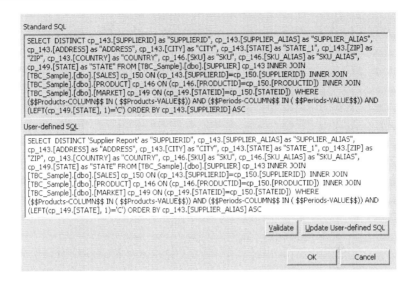

6. Copy the SQL Statement to Notepad. I like to format it to make it more readable.

```
SELECT  DISTINCT
cp_143.[SUPPLIERID] as "SUPPLIERID",
cp_143.[SUPPLIER_ALIAS] as "SUPPLIER_ALIAS",
cp_143.[ADDRESS] as "ADDRESS",
cp_143.[CITY] as "CITY",
cp_143.[STATE] as "STATE_1",
cp_143.[ZIP] as "ZIP",
cp_143.[COUNTRY] as "COUNTRY",
cp_146.[SKU] as "SKU",
cp_146.[SKU_ALIAS] as "SKU_ALIAS",
cp_149.[STATE] as "STATE"
FROM [TBC_Sample].[dbo].[SUPPLIER] cp_143
INNER JOIN [TBC_Sample].[dbo].[SALES] cp_150
ON (cp_143.[SUPPLIERID]=cp_150.[SUPPLIERID])
INNER JOIN [TBC_Sample].[dbo].[PRODUCT] cp_146
ON (cp_146.[PRODUCTID]=cp_150.[PRODUCTID])
INNER JOIN [TBC_Sample].[dbo].[MARKET] cp_149
ON (cp_149.[STATEID]=cp_150.[STATEID])
WHERE ($$Products-COLUMN$$ IN ( $$Products-
VALUE$$))
AND ($$Periods-COLUMN$$ IN ( $$Periods-VALUE$$))
AND (LEFT(cp_149.[STATE], 1)='C')
ORDER BY cp_143.[SUPPLIERID] ASC
```

We really don't need supplier ID, but I would like to have the rows reflect that this is the supplier report. So change the line cp_143.[SUPPLIERID] as "SUPPLIERID" to 'Supplier Report' as "SUPPLIERID" and change the Order by at the end to be Supplier_Alias (we can't order by a literal).

7. Replace cp_143.[SUPPLIERID] as "SUPPLIERID" to 'Supplier Report' as "SUPPLIERID".

8. Change the Order by at the end to be Supplier_Alias:

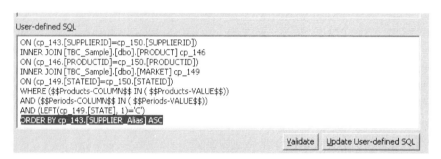

It is a little painful as the box does not have scroll bars, but if you move your cursor in the box it will move through the code.

9. When done, press the Validate button.

10. If you have no errors, save the changes by clicking on the Update User-defined SQL button.

11. If you did have errors, look at the details of the error message and try to figure out the issue. The messages can be cryptic.

12. Once the SQL validates, click OK to leave the screen:

13. Check the box for Use User Defined SQL to tell the system to use the User defined SQL instead of the standard SQL:

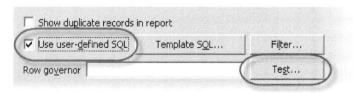

Next, test out the changes.

14. Click the Test button.

15. Using 100-10 as the SKU and Jan for the month, your report should look like:

Intersection				Column Value					Show	
SKU				100-10						
Month				Jan						

Maximum rows to display [20]

Resulting report

SUPPLIERID	SUPPLIER_ALIAS	ADDRESS	CITY	STATE_1	ZIP	COUNTRY	SKU	SKU_ALIAS	
Supplier Report	High Tech Drinks	1344 Crossman Ave	Sunnyvale	California	94675	USA	100-10	Cola	
Supplier Report	High Tech Drinks	1344 Crossman Ave	Sunnyvale	California	94675	USA	100-10	Cola	
Supplier Report	High Tech Drinks	1344 Crossman Ave	Sunnyvale	California	94675	USA	100-10	Cola	

16. When done, close this screen, then save and close the report. It is effective immediately.

If you'd like, jump back into Excel and Smart View to give the report a test drive.

"Did you just see that!?!" Edward yells again, my ears now ringing. "I thought for sure the drill through would never work."

CREATING A URL BASED DRILL THROUGH REPORT

URL based reports start out the same way as Relational Drill-through reports do. We name them and set up the Context or hierarchy levels where the drill through report is available. The difference in URL based reports is found on the Report Contents tab. For URL reports, we supply a URL up to 256 characters and pass parameters to the URL. Studio is nice to us in that it gives us three templates to help us up set up the URLs properly. The samples supplied are for standard, FDM and OBI URLS. Let's do a simple URL report.

1. Create a new report like you did for the relational report and name it URL_Report.
2. Select Product and Periods as the Hierarchies on the Context tab.
3. Set SKU and Month as the selectable levels (if you need step by step directions, look at the section on Relational Drill Through):

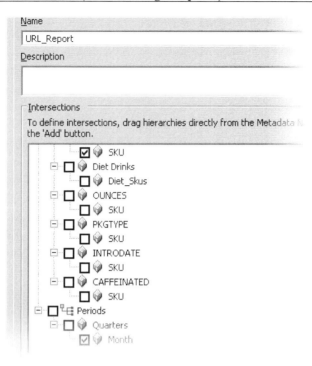

4. Switch to the Report Contents tab and select URL as the Drill-through report type.

   Notice the three different templates available: Sample URL Template, FDM URL Template, OBI URL Template.

5. Click on each one to see what it looks like.

6. Select Standard URL Template:

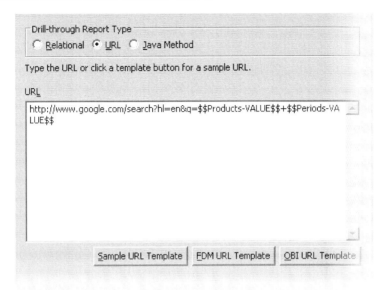

7. Notice the URL added the $$Products-Value$$ and $$Periods-Value$$ variables. They will get replaced with values when the URL is launched based on the intersection. Add to the end of the URL+Essbase+Sample+Basic.
http://www.google.com/search?hl=en&q=$$Products-VALUE$$+$$Periods-VALUE$$+Sample+Basic

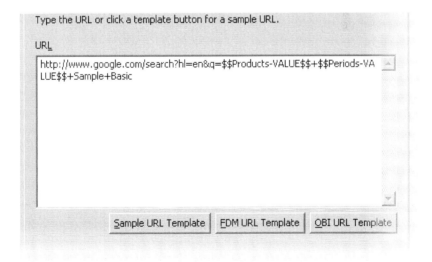

8. Switch to the Associations tab and associate to TBC_Sample.
9. Save and close the report.

A nice feature is the changes we make are immediate; we don't have to redeploy the Essbase cube to see the new drill through report.

10. Go to Excel and Smart View.
11. Create a report as shown below:

	A	B	C	D	E	F	G	H	I	J	K	L	M
1			Jan	Feb	Mar	Apr	May	Jun	Jul	Aug	Sep	Oct	Nov
2	Cola	Margin	2972	2935	2997	3099	3235	3578	3709	3734	3292	2985	29
3	Diet Cola	Margin	12	1267	1285	1334	1353	1399	1493	1389	1232	1229	11
4	Caffeine Free Cola	Margin		Drill-through:						490	568	557	56
5	Old Fashioned	Margin	1	\'TBC_Sample'\'Drill Through Reports'\'Suppliers'						2081	1886	1944	188
6	Diet Root Beer	Margin	1	\'TBC_Sample'\'Drill Through Reports'\'URL_Report'						1899	1784	1758	168
7	Sasparilla	Margin	821	830	848	854	876	846	884	793	780	776	78
8	Birch Beer	Margin	469	560	489	524	474	607	475	459	503	718	66
9	Dark Cream	Margin	1921	1992	2013	2190			0	2390	2035	2047	2124
10	Vanilla Cream	Margin	622	633	642	690	Scenario		4	558	512	574	55
11	Diet Cream	Margin	1704	1735	1725	1724	Market		5	1915	1748	1835	17
12	Grape	Margin	1633	1654	1662	1659	Refresh		5	1898	1727	1716	15
13	Orange	Margin	1442	1463	1470	1514	1573	1600	1619	1610	1588	1500	144
14	Strawberry	Margin	476	515	515	525	530	515	539	520	469	547	55
15	Diet Cola	Margin	1228	1267	1285	1334	1353	1399	1493	1389	1232	1229	11
16	Diet Root Beer	Margin	1747	1786	1810	1800	1834	1858	1899	1899	1784	1758	166
17	Diet Cream	Margin	1704	1735	1725	1724	1723	1795	1835	1915	1748	1835	17
18	Products	Margin	17378	17762	17803	18242	18618	19457	20012	19736	18124	18186	17

If you click on a data cell, notice that you now have two reports listed.

12. Assuming you are on Smart View 11.1.2, drill into the report.

Since there are multiple reports, you have to select which one you want.

13. Select URL_Report and click Launch:

The Google search screen should appear with info based on the product, period and Essbase Sample Basic:

"Did you just see that!?!" Edward's voice in a high pitched squeak. "Impossible... I thought it was impossible for sure."

Thankfully the crowd stood up and cheered at the stunts, drowning out Edward's loud annoying observations. Everyone, like Edward, was astonished at how easy our professional stunt men make drill through look. In fact it is easy, but most of the audience would never know. They would rely on others to create the drill-through for them.

CHAPTER 11:
THE THEME PARK

A lot of information had been given to Edward and Tracy, creating Essbase cubes and drill through reports from start to finish using Essbase Studio. I decided to give them some time to enjoy themselves in our theme park. It was originally called Dimensions Land, and later changed names to Solutions City, and currently is called Larry's Open World of Spinning Cubes (man, that is a long name). Nothing impresses a potential client more than getting their stomach turned inside out. I set them loose and we met back a few hours later. They were giddy as trying to compare their favorite attractions:

- The Unpatched Software House of Horrors (ever used a new release? It's terrifying.)
- The Scope Change Rocket to the Moon (jjust keeps going up until you suddenly free-fall back to Earth)
- Test-a-Whirl (guaranteed to make you vomit)
- Star Schema (one of those rides that throws the riders every which way to Sunday)
- Excel Hell (dark ride through the 7 circles of most financial analyst's lives)
- The Life Cyclone Management coaster (you start out in one place and who knows where you'll end up)
- Eddie and the Consultants: The Musical (a stage show showing in the theme park)
- It's a Small Cube After All (a zip roaring ride through ASO cubes)
- The XFactor OLAP Coaster (uncharted territories in coasters and space using XOLAP)

Edward and Tracy told me this last ride was one of the most unique rides they had encountered with Essbase. We will talk about this "ride" in detail. XOLAP, or eXtended On Line Analytic Processing, uses Essbase to store its metadata (the outline) but uses the source relational system to store the data. When data is requested for a front end tool, Studio submits one or more queries to the relational source to get the data.

XOLAP LIMITATIONS

XOLAP can be a really scary ride if you don't understand its limitations before you begin. Knowing the secrets of XOLAP smoothes some of the sharp turns and drastic falls that can get you into trouble.

Since XOLAP has such a specialized usage, it is understandable that it also has usage restrictions. These restrictions include:

- You can't edit an XOLAP cube. To modify an outline you must create a new outline from Essbase Studio.
- You must create a new Essbase application/database every time you deploy. You cannot reuse an existing database.
- You cannot create a XOLAP cube if the cube schema uses derived text measures.
- XOLAP creates ASO cubes only.
- Duplicate member support is automatically turned on.
- Alternate hierarchies and attribute dimensions are supported, but you cannot have a hierarchy in an attribute dimension.
- XOLAP supports user-defined dimensions, but only one member of the dimension can be a stored member; all others must be formulaic.

There are also a number of things that are not supported for XOLAP models. These include:

- Ragged hierarchies
- Flat files
- Recursive hierarchies
- Calendar hierarchies
- Filters
- Text measures
- Multiple relational sources
- User defined members at level zero

I'm sure you are asking yourself, "If there are so many restrictions on XOLAP, why would I want to use it?"

Three words: Real Time Data.

With XOLAP you can have up to the second data (well, as close as the query takes to run) available for end-users. In addition, you build on the scalability of a large database. You may want to partition an XOLAP cube with other Essbase cubes to combine real time data with less volatile data:

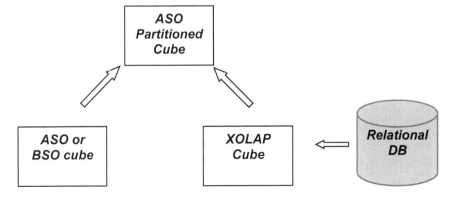

CREATING THE XOLAP DATABASE

Edward reluctantly stepped into the XOLAP coaster car to learn more about this new type of Essbase database. "I'm warning you now; I may just puke everywhere by the time this is over." He lamented. I assured him the ride was gentler than he thought. The ride operator pulled a lever and we are off to create an XOLAP cube:

1. Create a new minischema from the TBC_Sample **relational** source with the following tables:
    *   SalesFact
    *   Family
    *   Market
    *   Population
    *   Product
    *   Region

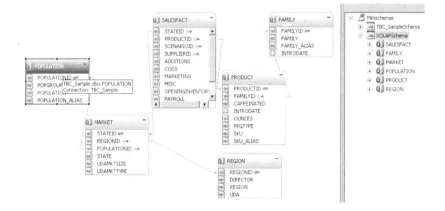

2. Add the SalesFact table to the members in the Metadata navigator (drag the SalesFact table from the Data Source or Minischema to the Members folder):

3. Delete everything except COGS, Marketing, Misc, Payroll, Sales and Transdate:

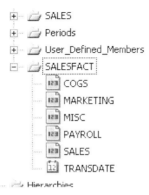

4. Create a new Hierarchy. Name it Periods1 and put in TRANSDATE from the SALESFACT table as its hierarchy:

5. Create a new Cube Schema called XOLAP. Add the members from SalesFact to the Measures:
   - SALES
   - COGS
   - MARKETING
   - PAYROLL
   - MISC
6. Add the following hierarchies:
   - Periods1
   - Scenario
   - Market
   - Products

We are re-using existing hierarchies. This saves us time and work effort.

7. Click Next and check Create Essbase Model. Notice that you cannot override system generated accounts dimension. This is because you have multiple items in measures. Click Finish:

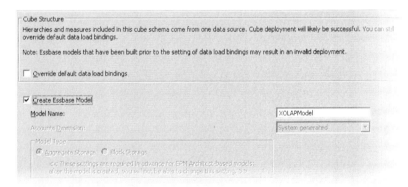

8. Edit the properties of theEssbase model named XOLAPModel.
9. For the model, set the Type to be XOLAP Model.

Notice how it sets Aggregate Storage Model and Duplicate Member name support:

Last deployed: [   ]

☑ Aggregate storage model

☑ Duplicate member name support

☐ Use Unicode character set

☑ XOLAP Model

10. Reorder the dimensions so they will be in this order:
    - Accounts
    - Periods1
    - Scenario
    - Market
    - Products

11. Set the following properties for the model:

Dimension/Member	Change	Tab
XOLAPModel	Add the Default Alias	Alias
Accounts/Accounts	Set the dimension name for the cube to Measures	General
	Set the Data storage to Label Only	Info
Periods1/Periods1	Set the name in cube to Periods	General
Periods1/Periods1	Set the Dimension type to Time	Info
Periods1/Periods1	Set Dimension storage to dense (This is dumb. It is the only to get rid of a warning message.)	Info
Scenario/Scenario	Set the Data storage to Label Only	Info
Products/Products	Set the Hierarchy settings to Multiple Hierarchies	Outline Build
Products/Products	Set the Duplicate	Outline Build

Dimension/Member	Change	Tab
	member settings to Do not move Duplicate members	
Products/Diet Drinks	Set the Consolidation to ignore (~)	Info
Products/Ounces	Set as a numeric attribute	General
Products/PkgType	Set as a string attribute	General
Products/Introdate	Set as a date/time attribute	General
Products/Caffinated	Set as a Boolean attribute	General

12. Apply the changes and verify the outline. Then close the model editor.

13. Deploy the cube using the cube deployment wizard. Give the application and database the name XOLAP. Click Next.

Tip!

Remember, you can't reuse XOLAP applications. You have to use a new one each time. If necessary, delete the application before deploying it from Studio.

14. Notice that the options for task type only allow you to build an outline. Choose that. Also notice you can't do an incremental build of the outline. Click Finish:

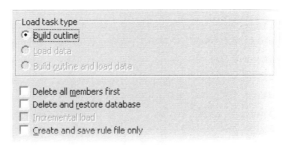

15. Hopefully the cube deploys correctly and you get the following message. Click OK:

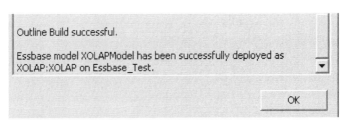

16. To test that we really have an XOLAP Model, go into EAS. Select the XOLAP application then database and examine the properties on the Statistics tab. Notice the input–level data size is 0, as are a number of other statistics:

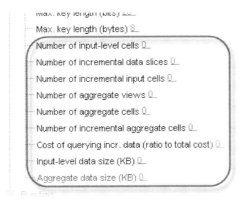

Now let us see if we can retrieve data from this empty database. Open Excel and Smart View and connect to the XOLAP database. Do an ad-hoc report. Notice that you have numbers even though the cube is empty:

	A	B	C	D	E	F	G
1			Actual	Budget	Scenario		
2	Jan 1 2000 12:00AM	SALES	102.9	295	102.9		
3	Jan 1 2000 12:00AM	COGS	42.68	121	42.68		
4	Jan 1 2000 12:00AM	MARKETING	13.53	28.3	13.53		
5	Jan 1 2000 12:00AM	PAYROLL	20.9	38	20.9		
6	Jan 1 2000 12:00AM	MISC	0.76	0	0.76		
7	Jan 1 2000 12:00AM	Measures	102.9	295	102.9		
8	Jan 2 2000 12:00AM	SALES	70.3	8.6	70.3		
9	Jan 2 2000 12:00AM	COGS	52.32	3.4	52.32		
10	Jan 2 2000 12:00AM	MARKETING	15.83	0.6	15.83		
11	Jan 2 2000 12:00AM	PAYROLL	16.36	1.7	16.36		
12	Jan 2 2000 12:00AM	MISC	0.76	0	0.76		
13	Jan 2 2000 12:00AM	Measures	70.3	8.6	70.3		

Tracy and Edward were speechless (and thankfully Edward did not vomit everywhere). This was truly one of the most amazing rides they had been on. Normally I would have ended the tour on this high note and brought them back to my office to close the deal, but I knew Tracy would want more. I was in a good mood, so I decided to go the distance and give them the director's cut with extra footage. We were going to go into the darkest, dankest cave of the Studio. We were going to go to Studio

Operations. No one ever went there. These guys worked all night and never showered. We just slipped pizza boxes under the door for them once in a while.

CHAPTER 12: STUDIO OPERATIONS

As we walked to Studio Operations, I explained to Edward and Tracy that this was the central nerve station for the entire studio. From here all the rides, electrical, water, waste and other things were controlled - for the entire studio, not just the theme park. I let them know that the entire operation was run by a character named Al who was with us for over 17 years. He remembered when Essbase was not owned by Hyperion. Somehow the name was fitting for the position.

I brought Edward and Tracy through tunnels and paths that twisted and turned between pipes and wires and entered the central nervous system of the studio. And there sat Al.

So deep in the bowels of the studio and given the way I painted the picture, my two tag-a-longs expected to see a grizzled old grungy grip in overalls with the butt of a stogie clenched between his teeth. Al was nothing of the sort - he was a tall man in a suit and tie sitting behind an immaculate console in a room that was so clean you could eat off the floor.

Al jumped up and greeted us with open arms like an Italian grandmother squeezing tomatoes. I guess it really was lonely down here. I pulled out of his boa constrictor-like grip and, to distract him from crushing Edward and Tracy, I asked him to explain what Studio Operations did.

Al eased his grip and Tracy was finally able to gasp in a breath or two. His smile was catching; you could tell he enjoyed his job in the trenches of Essbase management.

Al explained that Studio Operations was the control center behind the studio. There were a lot of functions of operations, including:

- Keeping track of what artifacts were used where and when. It was something he called lineage (why did that sound familiar?).
- Exporting and importing models, connections and artifacts.
- Migration from an older entity EIS which was being phased out.
- Automating of processes.
- Like in a James Bond thriller, controlling security.
- Setting properties that controlled the entire Studio environment.

- New to version 11.1.2.2 the ability to resync models due to hierarchy and schema changes.

Before he could renew his death like grip on us, I asked Al to elaborate on these functions.

LINEAGE

Edward was interested in Lineage. He figured I was going to tell him all about his ancestors. He thought he was a descendant of the Dread Pirate Roberts. Al chuckled at this, but Edward was not far off in understanding what Lineage is in Essbase Studio. Lineage is the ability to track the usage of artifacts within Studio forward or backward. For example, you can select a dimensional element and track back to see what table it comes from and forward to see what Essbase models it is used in. It is extremely handy, especially if you need to make a change to that element. Before you make a change, you want to see what other artifacts need to be changed, or if you need to delete a column from a table

One important reason to use linages is when you need to delete columns or even complete tables from your data source. If that column is used anywhere: Aliases, dimension members, hierarchies, Essbase models, these items have to be deleted before you can delete the column. I recommend working backward. Start deleting from Cube Models and Alias sets. Then work backward from there, deleting cube schemas, hierarchies, dimension elements and minischemas in that order based on where lineage shows you where the column is used.

Lineage is graphical and is easy to use. Al described a pretty picture of lineage, so Tracy and Edward wanted to see it. Al was quick to comply with their wishes.

1. From the Hierarchies folder, right click on the Market Hierarchy and select Show Lineage:

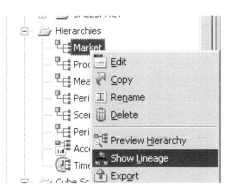

The following will appear in the work pane:

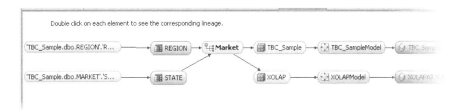

2. Hover the cursor over the Region bubble and you will see more detailed binding information for that artifact:

We see that Market is used by the TBC_Sample cube schema, but we want to know what else is used by that schema.

3. To see that, double click on the TBC_Sample cube schema bubble:

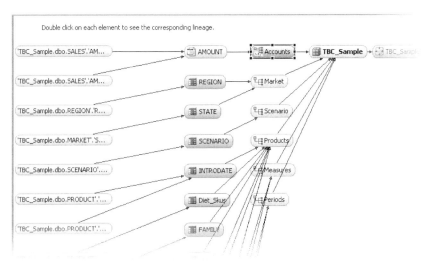

4. Now double click on Accounts to see where it is used.

Also notice when you do this that Studio has added tabs along the top of the work pane to allow you to navigate between your selections. To close a tab, click on the white X on the tab:

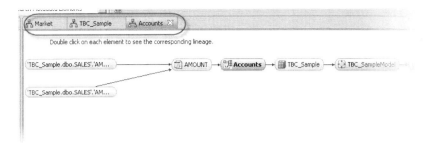

You can also move the artifacts around by clicking on them with the left mouse key and dragging them to where you want them. Give it a try. If the diagram is too large or you want to look more specifically at an area, you can zoom in or out by right clicking anywhere in the diagram and selecting the zoom feature you want:

Finally, if the diagram is large, you can open the thumbnail viewer (see circled item above) to see the entire work pane. Moving the blue shaded rectangle moves the work pane to that area of the work pane:

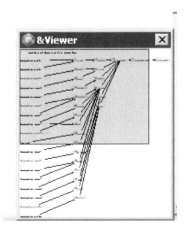

You can use the zoom in, zoom out and thumbnail viewer in minischemas and Essbase models as well.

Tip!

EXPORTING AND IMPORTING

Now that Edward and Tracy fully understood lineage, Al went on to talk about the importance of exporting and importing the database. It turns out you can export the entire catalog from within Studio or you can selectively choose items to export. When you export artifacts, they are exported to a location of your choosing in an XML format.

Exporting the Entire Catalog

1. Within Essbase Studio, select File>> Export:

2. Click Browse and designate a location for the export file:

3. Click Save:

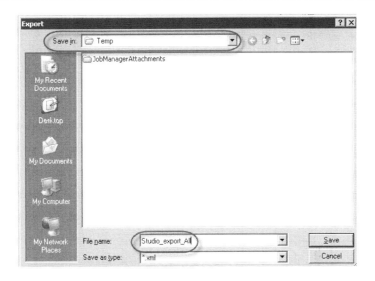

4. If you like, enter a description for the export.
5. Select Export entire catalog. If you want to include the Essbase models with the cube schemas (I'm not sure why you wouldn't), check that box.
6. Click OK:

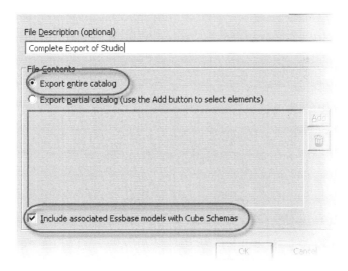

While it is working you will get a moving bar (something that looks like KITTS' grill from Knight Rider):

When complete, you will get the message:

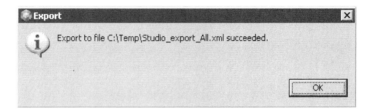

7. Click OK.

Exporting Selected Studio Items

While it is easy to export the entire model, sometimes you have just made a few changes to specific objects and need to migrate them between systems. Other times you want to try changes and be able to revert back to original objects. Exporting selected items allows you to do both of these. As a sample, we're going to export the TBC_Sample connection.

1. Select TBC_Sample data source and right click.
2. Select Export Connection:

For other objects, the menu selection is just Export.

The same screen for a full export appears, but with the artifact you selected included (in our case the TBC_Sample connection). Like for a full export, browse and find a location where you want to put the file and give it a name.

3.   Click Browse and designate a location and enter a file name for the export file:

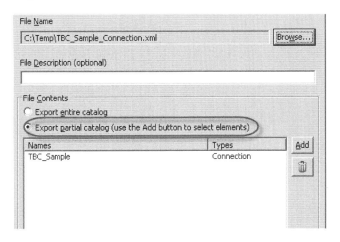

4.   If you want to add more artifacts to export, click on the Add button

 then select the artifact type you want to Add:

5.   In our case, we don't want any additional artifacts; just click OK.
6.   The XML file will be saved.
7.   Navigate to the directory where you saved the XML file and open it with Wordpad to see the format:

```
<?xml version="1.0" encoding="UTF-8" ?>
<objects>
    <exportType>individual</exportType>
    <serverVersion>Version 11.1.2.0.00, Build 590, March 26 2010.</serverVersion>
    <connection>
    <incrementalCreation>false</incrementalCreation>
    <info><![CDATA[]]></info>
    <name><![CDATA[TBC_Sample]]></name>
    <path><![CDATA[\]]></path>
    <schema><rules>
    <rule>
    <ruleKind>JOIN</ruleKind>
    <primarySources>
        <primarySource><![CDATA[connection : \'TBC_Sample'::'TBC_Sample.dbo.FAMILY']]></primarySource>
    </primarySources>
    <foreignSources>
        <foreingSource><![CDATA[connection : \'TBC_Sample'::'TBC_Sample.dbo.PRODUCT']]></foreingSource>
    </foreignSources>
    <expression><![CDATA[connection : \'TBC_Sample'::'TBC_Sample.dbo.FAMILY'.'FAMILYID' == connection : \'TB'
    <modality>FULL</modality>
</rule>
    <rule>
    <ruleKind>JOIN</ruleKind>
    <primarySources>
        <primarySource><![CDATA[connection : \'TBC_Sample'::'TBC_Sample.dbo.SUPPLIER']]></primarySource>
    </primarySources>
    <foreignSources>
        <foreingSource><![CDATA[connection : \'TBC_Sample'::'TBC_Sample.dbo.SALES']]></foreingSource>
    </foreignSources>
    <expression><![CDATA[connection : \'TBC_Sample'::'TBC_Sample.dbo.SUPPLIER'.'SUPPLIERID' == connection :
    <modality>FULL</rule>
```

Importing

Tip!

It is important to know that you cannot selectively import from an XML file. You must import all the contents.

Importing Studio objects is just as easy as exporting them. Why would you want to import? Perhaps you want to migrate models between Development and Prod. You would export from development then import the model to prod. Also, as with the selective export, you can restore old objects after testing.

1. If necessary, copy or move the files you exported to the new server using the file transfer method of your choice -FTP, File copy, sneakerware, camel, etc.

2. From Essbase Studio, select File >> Import:

3. In the screen that appears, browse to the location of your export files and choose the file you want to import. In our case we want to import TBC_Sample_Connection.XML.
4. Select it and click Open:

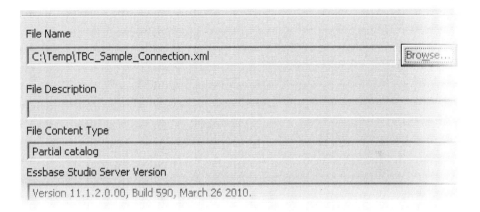

Notice that it gives you information about the type of export and version of Studio it was exported from.

5. Choose how you want to deal with existing elements. You can either select:

Selection	What it does
Check for elements and overwrite them	If the element already exists in the Studio system database, overwrite it with information from the XML file.
Check for elements but do not overwrite them	If the element already exists in the Studio system database, use that entry and ignore the values from the XML file.
Do not check for elements; all elements are new	The Studio System database (Catalog) is created from the XML file.

We want to overwrite the elements if they exist, so choose the first option.

6. Choose Check for elements and overwrite them:

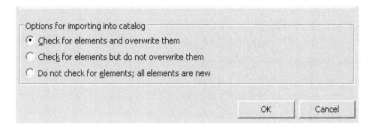

7. Click OK.
    If there were no problems with the import, the following screen will appear:

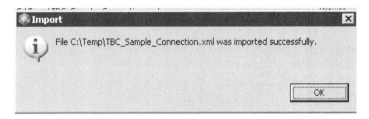

The objects should be successfully imported into the Essbase Studio environment.

UPDATING CUBE LINKAGE

Al explained that when the animators get an Essbase model, it is associated in their studio instance, but once created, there are times when you want to change that association to another instance. Two examples of the usefulness of this are: 1) Drill-through reports can be directed to a different Studio instance and model for load balancing and 2) in XOLAP models, update the login information so you don't have to recreate the model or cube

In Cube Linkage you can change:

*   The Studio server and port used to deploy a cube
*   The model a cube is based on
*   The Login information for a data source which built a cube
    To update the Linkage,
    Let's look at Cube linkage
1. From the Tools menu, select Update Cube Linkage:

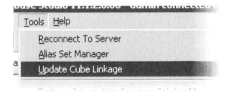

In the screen that appears, navigate to the Essbase Server/cube application/database you want to change. In our case it is Essbase_test/TBC/Sample.

2. Highlight Essbase_test/TBC/Sample and click on the Update button:

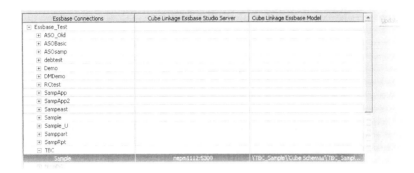

In the dialog that appears, you can change the Studio Server the cube connects to and, once you select the server, you can select what model the cube connects to. In our case we really don't want to make any changes so click Cancel. Then close the Cube Linkage dialog box:

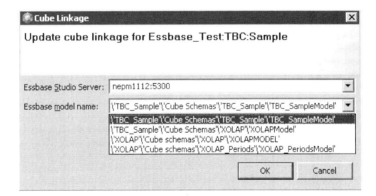

AUTOMATION

Al was all set to tell Tracy and Edward about the great things you can do when you deploy a cube, but I had to stop him. I let Al know that Other Ed had stolen his thunder by showing how to save the Deploy MaxL command from the cube deployment wizard. Rather than get his feelings hurt, Al expanded on what Other Ed had told them. In addition to using the deploy MaxL command to build your cubes, you can integrate the Studio created load rules within your other processes. You can use the dim build rules and data load rules in EAS or in MaxL scripts. Al did emphasize that the Deploy command is the preferred way to build and refresh cubes. It has built in functionality to make building, rebuilding and loading cubes easy.

In addition, he let our two tourists in on a little secret. Other Ed had told them that you can't open the rules files Studio creates for building the metadata. What he did not tell them was you CAN open and modify the data load rules file. It will show you the columns and connections it is using and you can modify it.

From EAS, you can open and edit a rules file created by Essbase Studio to load data:

SECURITY

Al turned the lights down low, put on his night vision goggles, started playing "Somebody's Watching You" by Chaka Khan and pressed a button and down came what he called the cone of silence. Al took security way too seriously, especially as all he was doing was telling us how security worked with respect to Essbase Studio.

He explained that, like the other Hyperion products, security is administered through Shared Services. In order to have access to Studio, you have to be provisioned for it. There are 4 roles can be assigned for Studio accessibility and a fifth role that allows you to provision other people in Studio. The roles are:

- cpAdmin. This is the Administrator role. It allows you to perform all Studio tasks, including cube deployment and executing Drill-through reports.
- cpDM. DM stands for Data Modeler and allows you to perform all metadata creation and maintenance related tasks. Like cpAdmin, it allows you to deploy cubes and execute Drill-through reports.

- cpDSAdmin. The Data Source Administrator role lets you do tasks related to data source connections and allows you to execute Drill-through reports.
- cpViewer. This role lets you look at the Studio model artifacts but not change them. Its main purpose it to allow access to execute Drill-through report:

In addition to these roles, if a user has cpAdmin or cpDM it is important to realize they also must be given certain other roles. This access is necessary to allow them to deploy the cubes to Essbase. Two of these roles are required and two are optional. These roles include:

- Shared Service Project manager
- Essbase create/delete application
- Essbase Administrator (optional)
- Shared Services Administrator(optional)

Tip!

Studio users who deploy cubes inherit access to the cubes in Essbase; other users may have to be provisioned to have access to the cubes.

SERVER.PROPERTIES FILE

Al had become very friendly with Tracy and Edward and before I knew it, he had revealed the deepest and darkest secret of Essbase Studio. He told them about the server.properties file. The server.properties file controls many of the aspects of the Studio. It is the brains behind the productions. The file is located in the directory (assuming 11.1.2): MIDDLEWARE_HOME/user_projects/epmsystem1/BPMS/bpms/bin.

A default file is created when you install Studio and is updated from the configuration manager. Al did not go into all 25 (currently) settings in the file; he did discuss some of his favorites.

- **server.datafile.dir**. This setting defines the root directory where flat files are stored. Be cautious of where you put this directory.

The path in non-unicode applications is limited to 121 characters. An example would be:

- C:\\EssbaseStudio\\text_file_sources\\tbc_txt
- When using backslashes you have to use two since the backslash is an escape character.
- **server.timeoutPeriod**. This is the amount of time in seconds the Studio console can remain idle before it disconnects. The default is 1 hour (3600 seconds).
- **server.essbase.streamingCubeBuilding.** A Boolean to describe how Studio should react during deployments. By default it is false, which means that during deployment, Essbase contacts the source directly using ODBC connections. In Streaming mode (true) Studio connects to the source and passes the information. Nonstreaming mode is faster.

Tip!

Starting in Studio 11.1.2.2, streaming mode is now in the Deployment wizard (and Deploy MaxL) instead of the properties file. It can be set independently for each deployment instead of globally.

- **server.sql.fetchSize**. The number of records in the JDBC fetch buffer. By default this is 1000 records.
- **server.readLockTimeOut.** This defines the number of seconds a process will wait before timing out when requesting information from the Studio catalog. By default it is 120 seconds. This setting is used in conjunction with server.writeLockTimeout. Certain actions when multiple users are on Studio can cause waits; these include creating or modifying metadata elements or data exploration, like creating or updating data sources.
- **server.writeLockTimeOut.** The amount of time in seconds a request will wait before timing out when trying to write to the Studio catalog database. This works with the read timeout and, like the read timeout, the default for it is 120 seconds.
- **server.runInBackground.** This setting determines whether the console should be visible. When set to true, the console runs in the background and no interaction with the console is possible. By default this setting is set to false, but on Unix systems it is automatically updated to True.

Al started humming his much loved song from the Sound of Music, "These Are a Few of my Favorite Things". He interrupted himself just long enough to tell Edward and Tracy that if they wanted to learn more about the settings, the Studio User Guide was the place to look.

Tip!

After changing the settings in the server.properties file, the Studio service must be restarted for them to take effect.

EIS MIGRATION

Essbase Studio provides a wizard to assist you in migrating existing Essbase Integration Services (EIS) models and metaoutlines into Studio.

"There are a number of limitations of EIS migrations,"Al warned before starting the steps for EIS migration. Some of the limitations include:

- Hybrid analysis metaoutlines are not supported.
- Unicode enabled models are not supported.
- All tables in your metaoutline must exist in the source database.
- The data types in the EIS model must match what is in the source db. If they do not match, the migration will fail.
- Metaoutlines with multiple ODBCDSN's are not supported.
- Studio does not support drill-through to alternate data sources. The metaoutline will be migrated, but the functionality will not.
- Recursive hierarchy drill-through reports will not be migrated. (Member name columns from the recursive hierarchies are not migrated.)

In addition to the above, certain properties are not migrated, including:

- Extra joins in tables
- User defined data load SQL
- UDAs
- Governors
- Metaoutline filters
- Unique key columns

Al finally explained that if the EIS and the Studio services were on different servers, you have to create an ODBC connection on the Studio Server to be able to connect to the EIS catalog.

With all these warnings Edward was not sure if he wanted to continue. Edward was sure if he started the migration a thousand volts would pass through his scrawny body when he started the process. Al assured him it was not that bad and proceeded to show them the migration wizard.

Most of you readers will not be able to follow along with the exercises unless you have an EIS system set up just like ours... which was not likely. So what Al is about to show you is more a demo than an exercise.

1. From the tools menu, select Essbase Integration Services Catalog Migration:

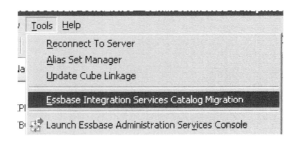

2. In the wizard that appears (no, it is not Merlin or Gandalf) enter in the ODBC DSN that is set up for the EIS system catalog.

3. Enter the user ID and password for the catalog and click on fetch models:

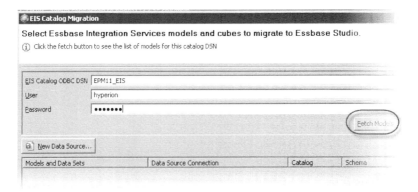

4. Next, if the data source(s) for the model(s) to be migrated don't exist, you have to create a new data source. This is similar to initially creating a data source. If necessary, click on the New Data Source button to create your new source:

5. Like any other data source, give the connection information and pick the tables and views to be included:

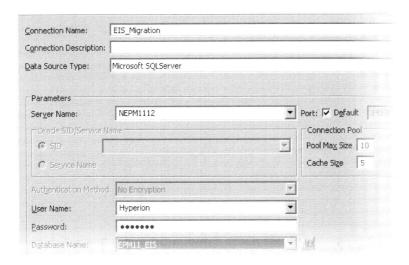

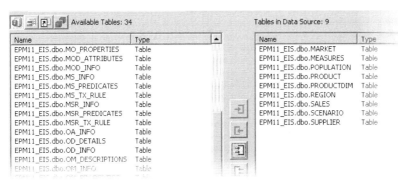

6. Select which model(s) and metaoutline(s) you want to migrate.
    Although they do not look like it, the columns for Data Source Connection, Catalog and Schema are all drop down boxes that you have to select something for.

7. Double click on the box and drop down the list. Select your data source, catalog and schema:

8. You now have to have a folder in the metadata navigator to put the migration results into.

9. Click the Browse button and either select an existing folder or create a new one. I created a new folder called EIS_Migration. (If I want I can always rename it later.)

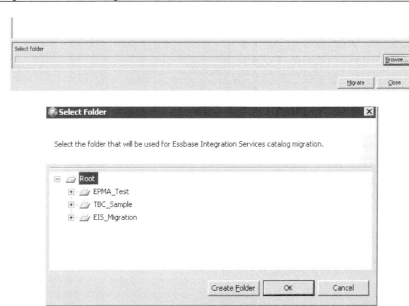

10. With all that completed, the Migrate button is now available. Click Migrate to start the migration process:

A status box will appear showing you the progress of your migration:

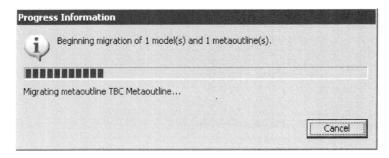

When the migration is complete, the progress box will disappear and you can view the migrated objects in the metadata navigator:

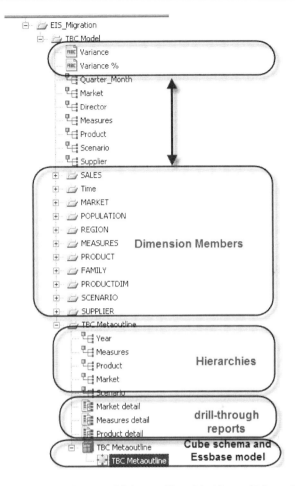

"How much simpler could it get?" said Al, as Edward stood there agape. The reality was it really was easy, as most things in Studio are.

RESYNCING ESSBASE MODELS

Al was giddy in explaining that prior to version 11.1.2.2 if you made changes to hierarchies or to cube schemas you had to completely rebuild the Essbase model for the changes to be enacted, However you did not know the model was out of sync with the Hierarchies. In Essbase Studio 11.1.2.2, you have visual clues and the ability to activate the changes without having to recreate the model properties. This allows you to keep out of sync models active to update when you have an open window of time and/or to ensure all models are updated at the same time. There are two different forms of synchronization Hierarchy and Cube Schema.

SYNCHRONIZATION FOR HIERARCHY CHANGES

When you change a hierarchy, if it is being used in an Essbase model, you will receive warnings about out of sync models and then have the ability to update the hierarchy. To illustrate this, we will modify the Years Hierarchy. One interesting thing about synchronization from hierarchy changes is that no matter how many hierarchies you change, when you synchronize, Essbase Studio only syncs the hierarchy you selected. So if you change three hierarchies, you have to run through the synchronization routine three times.

1. From the metadata navigator, expand the Hierarchies folder and edit the Years hierarchy.
2. Add the Year data element and move the Quarter and Month to be descendants of it (as shown below):

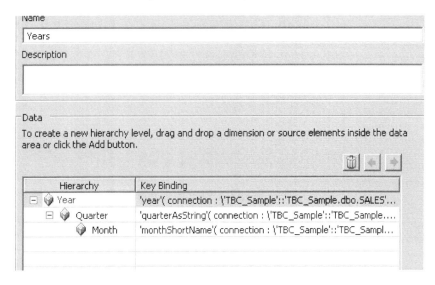

3. When you save the changes, the following message will appear:

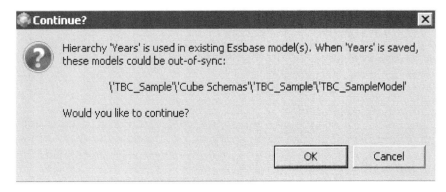

4. Click OK to save the Hierarchy.

5. Right click on the Hierarchy member and select Update-out-of-Sync Models:

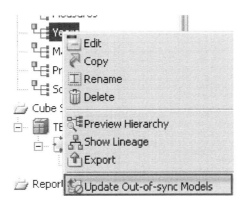

6. The following screen will appear. Select one or more models to Sync (Move from the left to right pane):

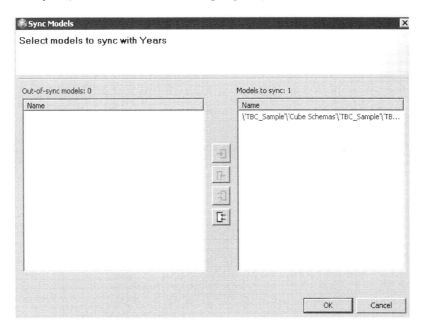

7. Click OK and the following message should appear:

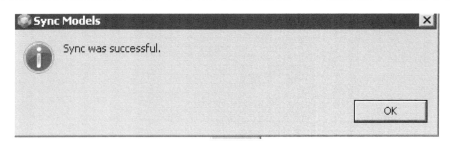

SYNCHRONIZATION FOR CUBE SCHEMA CHANGES

You will use cube schema resynchronization when you make changes to a cube schema. For example if you movie or replace dimensions in a cube schema, you need to resync your Essbase model. A nice feature is that Essbase Studio provides visual cues when a model needs to be synced. In the following example, we take the existing TBC_Sample cube schema and move the hierarchies around to force the resync.

1. Open the TBC_Sample cube schema .
2. Take the scenario dimension and remove it from the selected hierarchies list. If you built your cube schema like I did it will be the third item.
3. Re-add the Scenario to be the last item. Don't worry; you can move it around in the Essbase Model if you want. The following warning will appear.
4. Click OK to continue and save the changes:

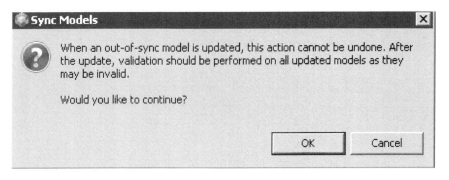

5. Click OK to continue and save the changes.
6. If you look at the Model(s) under the cube schema, you will see a little ghost busters symbol. This signifies that the model is out of sync:

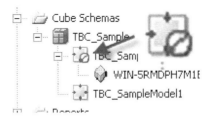

7. Right click on the model and select Update Out-of-Sync Model:

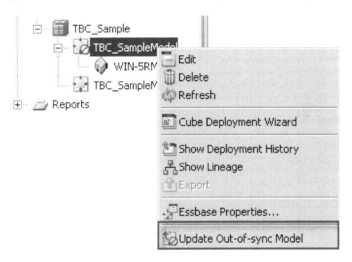

8. The following screen appears. Note: if you click on the cube schema, it gives you the option to update all of the models under the cube schema. If you click on the model you are only offered the model you selected.

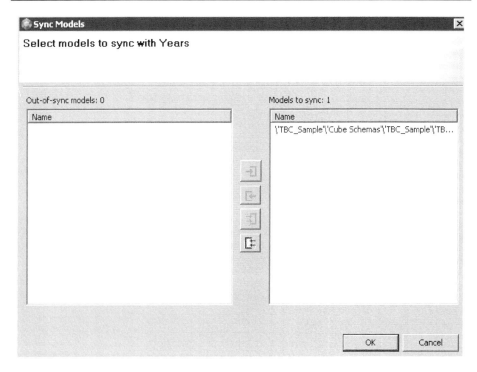

9. Move the desired model(s) to the Models to Sync pane and click OK.
10. When complete, the following message is displayed.

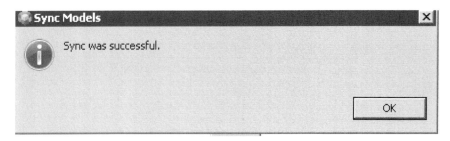

It was time to leave and we could all see the disappointment on Al's face. So Edward and Tracy agreed to one more hug. It lasted for 5 minutes. Then we snaked our way out through the maze and were once again feeling the fresh cool breeze on our faces as the tram rode along the back lot features.

The tram discarded us back at the dump I call my office, the place where this whole crazy tour began. We had a belly full of it and more. But I was still stumped. Tracy had taken more notes than an orchestra played in Beethoven's Fifth (that reminded me, where exactly was my office bottle) but Edward hadn't written a jot. I didn't know if he had a photographic memory or what. The reason soon came to light. It turned out Edward was more wired than a server cabinet. He had every gizmo and doodad to connect to his home planet on him. Modems, iCushion, you name it he had it. Oh, the light saber I gave him, turns out he had turned it into a super antenna and while on the tour, as we showed him how to do something in Studio, he mimicked it on his server with his data.

I was played for the sucker again. By the end of the trolley line, he'd built the mother of all wolverine applications. When I asked him, "How could you?" he replied, "Just like you've said throughout the tour -It was easy." The end of the tour line was a cemetery for my dreams.

So it seemed Essbase Studio had another blockbuster on its hands. The users couldn't wait for the premiere. The only shame is that I did not get to produce it and would not have the opportunity to pick up one of those little golden cigarette lighters named Oscar. With the reusability of what Edward had created, Tracy was sure there were plenty of sequels to come. Edward was brighter than I thought, but he was still a snot nosed punk. I was happy to have shown them Essbase Studio and even happier when they walked out that door so I could get back to my 100 proof lunch. Here's looking at you, kid.

APPENDIX A:
WHAT'S NEW IN ESSBASE STUDIO 11.1.2?

This book was written based on Essbase Studio 11.1.2 which added features and enhanced the 11.1.1.X versions significantly. If you are using the older versions you should be aware of a number of differences and limitations. I will attempt to detail most of the differences in the same order as if you were building a Studio model.

Data Sources

1. There are two significant impacts in Data source connections. During data source selection, Studio is required to explore the data source. In 11.1.1.X doing so would lock Studio catalog so in a multiuser environment; other users could not get to the catalog while data source creation was occurring.

2. In 11.1.1.X, changes to tables and views were not allowed. If a column was added, deleted or its data type was changed you could not update the data connection. If a table or view was also no longer in use, you could not remove it. To make a change, you had to start over. To remove the connection, you would first have to work backward deleting everywhere the columns were used first. Starting with Drill-through reports, Essbase models, Cube schemas, hierarchies, Dimension members, Alias and minischemas would all have to be removed, then you would delete the data source and recreate it, then rebuild the entire model.

3. Only the OBI semantic layer could be used as a source, the business layer could not.

Dimension Members

Text measures and text list mapping were not available.

Alias Sets

In 11.1.1.X you are limited to 10 alias sets instead of 32. You get even less if you are modifying the Essbase model properties to optimize data loading.

Cube Schemas

The order you placed hierarchies in a cube schema was the order they would show up in the Essbase cube. Once created, you could not move them around without rebuilding the Essbase model. Version11.1.2 allows ordering of the dimensions within the Essbase model.

Essbase Models

One of the biggest areas of frustration in the 11.1.1.X releases was with Essbase models. There were a number of limitations including:

1. Any change to a dimension member or hierarchy required you to completely rebuild the Essbase model.
2. There was no support for named generations or levels.
3. The model could put shared members before their stored version. While this caused warnings in BSO cubes, it would cause ASO cubes to fail to build.
   All of these issues have been corrected in 11.1.2.

Deployment

There were significant changes made to the deployment process in 11.1.2.

1. In 11.1.1.X when executing the deploy command, you could not have the deployment wizard create the deployment statement for you. For some, following the technical reference's MaxL commands was difficult and it had errors in syntax.
2. During a deploy from the Studio console, you had no visual cues as to what the deploy was doing. You only got a status box telling you the deploy was running.
3. You could not choose the type of connection to use for deployment. You were limited to the ODBC connection Studio created
4. Connections were single threaded with one physical connection per data source. You could not have connection pooling to improve performance

Drill-through

In 11.1.1.X drill-through on recursive hierarchies was not built in. If you were good with SQL you could write a user defined SQL but it was cumbersome to say the least.

Administration

The administration of Essbase Studio was more limited in prior version in a lot of ways including:

1. The install would not install Essbase studio as a windows service. To do so, you had to use third party software and undocumented or supported features.

2. There was no way to export or import parts of models. The only ways to move from one environment to another would be to back up the entire repository and more it to the new instance or rebuild on the new environment from scratch.

3. There was no support for Essbase clusters.

4. The lineage views were much slower and always showed two physical elements for every logical one.

5. SSL support was limited.

APPENDIX B:
WHAT'S NEW IN ESSBASE STUDIO 11.1.2.1?

Of course as soon as the book was published, Oracle released Essbase Studio 11.1.2.1. Does this mean that everything you have read has changed? Luckily, no, aside from some bug fixes, there is little in Essbase studio that has changed. This means the adventures of Edward and Tracy are still valid. We have not taken a new turn to drop them off a cliff somewhere. What is new and exciting? Read on and find out!

Essbase Studio Server and Catalog Upgrade

This release lets you upgrade from prior releases. Upgrading from Essbase Studio 11.1.2 is a no brainer, you just use the "Apply Maintenance Release" option in the EPM System installer. If you want to install from an earlier version, 11.1.1.3 is the only supported 11.1.X version to upgrade from. So if you are not on that version, first upgrade Studio to that version then upgrade to 11.1.2.1.

If you are upgrading Essbase from 9.3.1 or before, you need to upgrade to 9.3.3 instead. This is because these versions had security synchronization between Essbase and Shared Services.

OBIEE Business Model Support

In prior versions you could only connect to the Presentation layer of OBIEE. Now when you create an OBIEE connection, you are presented with a choice of the Presentation Layer or the Business Model. You can use the created metadata elements like elements from any other data source. It should be noted that Measures and Measure Hierarchies are not automatically created, but you can add the elements to the metadata navigator.

OBIEE Business Model Binding Rules

When OBIEE creates the hierarchies for you it builds the hierarchy based on primary keys. The problem with this is many primary keys are numeric IDs and would be meaningless member names. The developers have created a complex set of rules to insure this does not happen. These rules are for both the Key bindings and the Caption bindings.

Key Bindings

Remember these are used to connect tables together and for duplicate member name hierarchies. The rules are:

1. If there is a single primary key. The key is used as the binding
2. If there are several primary keys, the binding is the concatenation of all keys separated by underscores. If the keys are not of type string, they are converted to strings.
3. If there is no primary key, Essbase Studio does not create a dimension element for the dimension level.

Caption Bindings

Caption bindings are what Essbase actually uses as its member names. They certainly seem complicated. I'm glad the developers figured then out so I don't have to. To determine what to use Studio follows the following rules:

1. If the primary key is a string (not created by concatenating keys together, see #2 above), then Studio uses it as the key.
2. If the key binding expression is not a string, then the first OBIEE logical column that is a key column (not a primary key column), and has type of CHAR or VARCHAR, is used as a caption binding expression.
3. If the key binding expression is not a string, and there is no key column with type CHAR or VARCHAR, then the key binding conversion, .toString, is used as a caption binding expression.
4. If the binding expression is a string as a result of the concatenation of several primary keys, then the caption binding expression is the same as the key binding expression.

Cube Deployment from OBIEE

The new features guide for this release referees to Cube deployment from OBIEE. This in fact was never implemented.   SSL support for Studio connections

Essbase Studio can now be deployed to work in Secure Socket Layer (SSL) security. With this option, all communication between Essbase Studio, EPMA and the Essbase Server is encrypted. You specify SSL mode when you set up the connection to an SSL enabled Essbase server.

APPENDIX C: WHAT'S NEW IN ESSBASE STUDIO 11.1.2.2?

As time goes on, Essbase Studio keeps getting better and better. As you have read through the book, the tour had to take many detours due to changes in functionality and features. While most of the details of the new features are interspersed in the book, you can get s synopsis of them here.

Essbase Model resynchronization

In prior versions, when you made changes to metadata members, hierarchies and cube schemas, it required a resynchronization of your Essbase models. This meant recreating the properties in the Essbase model. Now you have the option (in multiple places) to update one or more models with the changes. This gives you flexibility to use old versions of the model until you want to change them. When you make changes, to a hierarchy for example, you get a warning message that Essbase models are out of sync. In addition, there is an icon showing you what models are out of sync. Items that would cause a resynchronize to be necessary include:

- A new hierarchy is added to a cube schema
- A hierarchy is removed from a cube schema
- A hierarchy is replaced with a different hierarchy in a cube schema
- A hierarchy is moved or repositioned in a cube schema
- A chain is added to a hierarchy
- A chain is removed from a hierarchy
- A chain is replaced in a hierarchy
- A chain is moved or repositioned in a hierarchy
- A chain in a hierarchy is edited
- A member is added to a hierarchy
- A member is removed from a hierarchy
- A member is replaced in a hierarchy
- A member is moved or repositioned in a hierarchy

When you resyncronize a hierarcy, only that hierarchy is modified even if you have made changes to multiple hierarchies. Hierarchies that are added or removed from a cube schema will not be resynced,

Tip!   See chapter 12 for details on how to resync models

Streaming options Is available in Cube deployment wizard

In prior releases, the streaming option is/was set in the server.properties file and was a global setting. In this version, you have the option to set this in the cube deployment wizard. This gives you more flexibility when you are deploying cubes. This option is disabled if you are using flat files, EPMA, or a mixed set of sources for deployment.

Minischemas are part of the Data sources

Since minischemas are really tied to data sources, the two have been combined in the data source tab (which has been renamed Data Source Navigator). Minischemas appear within the datasource tree.

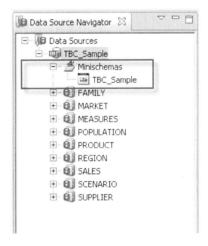

Alias Set Enhancements

In this release, the maintenance of Alias sets have been moved from the Tools menu into the Metadata navigator. This means they are treated like other metadata elements and can be moved, copied, exported, imported and occur in multiple locations. The name of alias sets can be replicated in multiple folders, so in the Essbase model properties, a new setting "Name in cube" has been implemented to create unique alias tables in an Essbase cube.

Streamlined Modeling of OBIEE Business Model Sources

The functionality has been enhanced so when you Create a data source connection to an OBIEE Business Model source, you are also given the option to create hierarchies cube schemas and Essbase models. Once created, you still have the ability to modify any of them.

Cube Deployment from OBIEE

When the last version was released, this was shown in the new features guide and I thought it was really cool. You could use OBIEE and it would spawn the required information to build the entire Studio model from Data source through Essbase Model and build the Essbase cube. This turned out to be a fantasy or at least premature in the documentation. So when the documentation appeared again in this version of the new features guide, I was more skeptical and contacted my friends in Studio development. I am sad to report, the feature was pulled before release, but the documentation was not updated. I guess it is something we still have something to look for in the future.

Support for Oracle RAC Data sources

When I did my first implementation of Studio, the client had an Oracle RAC instance. It took hours trying to figure out the right combination of setting to use in order to connect to it. Now with this setting, when you create a data source, you can specify it is an Oracle Rac instance and put in the nodes for that instance. It would have made my life so much easier if this were implanted before. Now you won't feel my pain.

GLOSSARY

Artifacts

Objects or individual items of information that are used or created by processes. For example, dimension members, columns, and hierarchies are all artifacts.

Cube Schema

In Essbase studio, the hierarchies and members that make up the logical Essbase model.

Data Source

A relational database, OBIEE, EPMA, an Essbase connection or flat files which are feeds an Essbase Studio model or are targets of the model.

Deployment

The process of building or loading data to an Essbase model from Essbase Studio. This can be done from either the wizard within Essbase Studio or from MaxL. MaxL has a new Deploy command specifically for this process.

Drill through

The process of obtaining detailed data, a URL or running a Java program from within an Essbase retrieval and passing cube information to that process based on the member or intersection

Dimension Elements

Distinct members which are created from data source columns. The elements are used to create hierarchies. Dimension Elements can be filtered, sorted and have functions applied to them to modify them.

Essbase Model

A graphical representation of the relationships between hierarchies and the fact table used to build an Essbase database. The Essbase Model is also where you edit the properties for creating the Essbase database. These properties include things like: Cube Type, Dense/sparse settings, member properties, aliases used, Formulas, Udas, consolidation properties, Account and time dimension properties, and transformations.

Hierarchies

The organization of elements used to create a structure or logical aggregation of members. Hierarchies are combined to create the structure of an Essbase database. In Essbase Studio there are three types of hierarchies: Standard, Measures, and Calendar. Introspection
The act of inspecting data sources to determine the relationship of those tables based on primary and foreign keys and to take those relationships to create hierarchies.

Metadata Elements

The items that appear in the metadata navigator which includes dimension elements, hierarchies, cube schemas and drill-through reports.

Minischema

A graphical representation of a subset of tables and views of a data source. This representation defines the relationship between the tables which represents logical subject area to be used in further modeling

Shared Services

Part of the Hyperion Foundation services, establishes a secure environment for all of the Hyperion EPM system components. Within Shared Services security is defined for users and groups.

Varying Attribute

An attribute association that changes over one or more dimensions. For example: sales reps that change products over time.

XOLAP

Extended On line Analytical processing utilizes an Essbase database that only stores metadata members and processes SQL queries to provide data from a relational source at query time. XOLAP is only supported in ASO cubes that are duplicate member enabled.

INDEX